Justice
in
Igbo Culture

Justice in Igbo Culture

UNIBEN STUDIES IN PHILOSOPHY
VOL. TWO

Nkeonye Otakpor
Department of Philosophy, University of Benin
Benin City, Nigeria

malthouse 𝓜𝓟

Malthouse Press Limited
Lagos, Benin, Ibadan, Jos, Port-Harcourt, Zaria

Malthouse Press Limited
43 Onitana Street, Off Stadium Hotel Road,
Surulere, Lagos, Lagos State
E-mail: malthouse_press@yahoo.com
malthouselagos@gmail.com
Tel: +234 (01) -773 53 44; 0802 600 3203

Benin City Ibadan Jos Lagos Port Harcourt Zaria

© Nkeonye Otakpor 2009
First Published 2009
ISBN 978 978 8422 03 7

Dedication

To my parents who kindly brought me into this beautiful, interesting, difficult but fascinating world.

To my father, late Ogbuefi Mordi Otakpor who taught me humility, patience, tolerance and moderation.

To my mother, Madam Ememogonjo Otakpor, though lacking in formal education, she is my most inspiring teacher. From her I learnt the value of hard work, perseverance, grace under pressure and self-effacing good humour. Most of all, I learnt the importance of family, friendship and commitment from her.

Finally, to my late aunt, Madam Onyemabeono Ngbonkwo Otakpor. We were very fond of each other. I miss her.

Acknowledgements

My interest in law, particularly its philosophical antecedents, dates back to my undergraduate school programme in the University of Leuven, Belgium. There I had the opportunity of receiving lectures in philosophy of Law from Professor Jan. M. Brokman.

At graduate school, Essex University, in England, I was again fortunate to have been taught legal theory by Professor David Robertson. The late Prof. Bo Sarlvik was my greatest source of encouragement. He was more than my teacher. He was a mentor and a friend.

My classmates and schoolmates in Leuven and Essex were more than just that. We were like kith and kin. We shared our joys and sorrows as students in an environment very far away from home. We were all buoyed by the exuberance of youth but united in one thing; the pursuit of knowledge. In this pursuit we held together like a chain.

Among the many are late Frank Asike who would have been happy to read this manuscript and offer his often chilly comments. I thank Pat Asakome, Emmanuel Omanukwue, Chris Manus, Mrs Manus, Fabian Essiet, Joe I. Omoregbe, Atanasius Ibanga, Sam Akanimo, Joe Asike, Rev. Polycarp Ndugbu, Rev. Abanuka and the late Mark Awuluorah, for their love, friendship, encouragement and understanding.

There are other people, colleagues in this university and elsewhere, with whom I discussed this book project and whose ideas and suggestions made the difference when it mattered most: Vincent O. Adepoju, Lawrence Atsegbua and Emeka Chianu of this University. Chianu deserves special thanks for his suggestions for corrections, particularly of chapters five and six.

I also wish to thank Bert A. Okolo and Diokpa M.A. Onwuejeogwu for their interest and kindness in reading the manuscript and in offering improvements and corrections which I have endeavoured to incorporate.

Without Robinson Eteghrara of the Vice-Chancellor's Office, who typed and retyped the manuscript through all its stages, this book would not be published.

This book would probably not have been written without the support and interest of many people in Aniocha North Local Government Area of Delta State. While space constraint would certainly not permit the listing of all those who contributed to this project the following are difficult to forget: Chief G. Nkemnacho, late Chief Fidelis Nwanze, Chief Chris Biose, Okeleke Ekpei, Isikwe Adigwe, Andy Ebulokwu, Eziuche Okolie, Ikpeamanam Anene, my uncle and head of Maidor family, Ogbuefi Oteiwe Otakpor.

The palace officials in the towns and villages I visited in order to observe proceedings were wonderful. I thank them all.

The Editor-in-Chief of *AMAN, Journal of Society, Culture and Environment* kindly permitted the use of my essay earlier published in Volume 5, Numbers 1 and 2, 1985, pp. 66-77 of that journal. Selections from that essay are part of the materials used in Chapter six.

I thank my wife and our children: Chibuzor, Emefienem, Echezonam, Uzodinma, and Jebose, for their interest, support and understanding.

N.O.   *May 2008*
Benin City

Contents

Chapter 1

The universality of law and order

There has existed the naïve assumption that until the unsolicited advent of colonialism, the so-called "noble and savage" tribes had no legal system worthy of attention. The Igbo people were not exempted from this assumption.

This assumption was not restricted to the legal domain. It was sweeping enough to encompass everything and anything closely associated with the "primitive savage" tribes of Africa, Asia and Latin America. Thus their philosophy, history, art, music and dance, language, religion, political system and government, etc., were accorded an inferior status in comparison with those of Europe and North America.

It is against the background of this assumption that Radcliffe-Brown argued that "some simple societies have no law, although all have customs which are supported by sanctions."[1] Marett did not spare a thought. According to him, "law is difficult to find in primitive societies because in a general way no one dreams of breaching the social rules."[2] For some, the existence of a political system is one thing that of law is another. Hence for Lucy Mair, "to have a political system did not necessarily entail having law."[3]

Some other people held the view that because there was no political authority, there was neither legal authority, nor legal sanction, nor law.

---

[1] A.R. Radcliff-Brown, *Structure and Function in Primitive Society*, London: Kegan Paul, 1976, p. 212.

[2] R.R. Marett, *Anthropology*, London: 1912, pp. 182-3.

[3] Lucy Mair, *An Introduction to Social Anthropology*, Oxford: Clarendon, 1970, p. 127.

For others, the fact that there were no courts meant that there was no law. Yet for some others, the absence of officials charged with legislative and judicial functions meant the absence of law.

There may have been an absence of accredited and recognized legal authorities and institutions in the so-called primitive societies, but this did not mean the absence of law and order.

This time honoured view that non-Europeans evolved no credible worthwhile systems was nurtured and sustained with the infamous claim that only Europeans and their siblings reason, others do not: Europeans have reason, Africans have emotion. Simply put, the claim was racially-inspired.

The Europeanness of reason is not a superficial linguistic bias. It lies deep in European belief system, consciousness and philosophical traditions. This is not to say that there is, indeed, a distinctly non-European criterion for reasonableness. It is to make a claim which is no less a scandal to the pretensions of "European reason". Racism is, supposedly, one of the things from which truly rational thought and endeavour is to prevent.

Yet, the aspiration to reason common to all, transcending the contingent historical circumstances which differentiate minds from one another, lies at the very heart of the philosophical heritage of mankind. To deny this, is an act of disownness.

I find the idea that there is one true reason (European) and one true objective reality existing for all people quite unacceptable. I accept that all people operate on the assumption that there is an objective reality. What I reject is that, that "reality" must be necessarily determined and measured by European standard and that once this is ascertained this reality is the same for everybody or should be the same for everybody. The language each of us speaks is not neutral; it is in itself a shaper of ideas.

Evidence from the different branches of human knowledge indicates that there is no human group without its own history, language, custom, tradition, culture, political organization, religion, literature, mythology, law and philosophy. That any or all of these are undocumented is not to say that they are (or were) non-existent.

The English common law for example, like the Igbo customary law is not written, yet it is accorded recognition. Not only is it recognized; it is one of the foundations of the English legal system.

Law, like philosophy, religion, etc., emerges in all societies because of the common human problems which require the use of law for their resolution. The conflicts which appear among individuals within any society are inevitable and require some resolution. This search for solutions to human problems in the context of Igbo society did not proceed randomly and incoherently.

According to Roscoe Pound,

> "apparently there is some common fundamental element in human nature which calls forth the same jural institutions and gives rise to the same judicial puzzles under the most diverse circumstances and in the most distant times. The problems of legal history then, are recurrent problems. They are perennially recurrent problems."[4]

Granting the plausibility of this claim, the products of the human spirit, not only in politics, philosophy, myth, religion and poetry but in law as well, are not exactly similar. These are different from one culture to another.

The justification for this claim is not far-fetched. For man, the basic means of survival is reason. Reason is one thing that is peculiar to man. Rationality is man's foremost virtue. It enables man to identify and integrate the material provided by the senses.

This identification and integration is not uniform because rationality is field dependent. What this illustrates in a clear way is crucially important: the non-monolithic character of ways of life. There is no one single story about social life which is universal, and there is no specific, special and unique experience to be regarded as a model for others. Such models, wherever found, are acts of deliberate imposition.

Thus Goodman tells us that he is

> "convinced that there is no one correct way of describing or picturing or perceiving the world, but rather that there are many equally right but conflicting ways, and thus in effect, many actual worlds."[5]

We must, then, inquire into the standards compatible with such multiplicity of rightness, of rendering of all sorts, in all media, and in symbolic systems of every society.

Rorty has recently amplified this issue by his insistence on the historical embeddedness of all thought and that this affects our conception of reason as much as it does our conception of the nature of

---

[4] Roscoe Pound, "Making Law and Finding Law," *Ohio Law Reporter*, Vol. 13, 1915, p. 284.

[5] Nelson Goodman, *Ways of World Making*, Indianapolis-Indiana: Hackett, 1978, p. 14.

reality. In other words, there is no natural and neutral starting point, all explanations are bound up with historical and cultural traditions. Reason is not neutral, therefore there are no neutral terms with which to formulate and explain social facts.

Human beings are the beneficiaries of centuries of experience involved in the adjustment of relations, the ordering of conduct, and the explanation of social facts.

In using law to order conduct, even if subtly, the Igbo, like other communities, relied on three pillars which are inseparable:

a) the received centuries old traditional and authoritative ideals (*omenani*) of the socio-legal order which provide the guide and signpost to the resolution of conflict;

b) experience to determine what will achieve the resolution with "the least impairment of the scheme of interests as a whole, and with the least friction and waste;[6]

c) the employment of reason tested by experience and experience in itself measured and moderated by reason in order to determine whether conflicts are satisfactorily resolved, and furthermore, whether new developments can be accommodated without dislocation.

Against this background Soyinka's observation is apt, succinct and educative. According to him:

> "man exists in a comprehensive world of myth, history and mores; in such a total context, the African world, like my other 'world', is unique. It possesses, however, in common with other cultures, the virtues of complementarity. To ignore this simple route to a common humanity is, for whatever motives, an attempt to perpetrate the external subjugation of the black continent."[7]

On the other hand, there are certain basic values of human existence which are not only self-evident but universal. Finnis calls these values "human goods", and can be secured only through a system of law. The achievement of human goods requires reason and practical judgement

---

[6] Roscoe Pound, *Social Control Through Law*, New Haven: Yale University Press, 1942, pp. 109-110.

[7] Wole Soyinka, *Myth, Literature and the African World*, Cambridge: University Press, 1976, p. xii.

in conjunction with a system of law.

Human existence, whatever it means and wherever it is found, requires for its flourishing a legal system of some sort. Individual members of the human family as well as the family itself require a system of law if they are to attain their full potential.

Finnis enumerated seven of such irreducibly basic human goods. While there are obviously many more of such goods, these seven are the irreducible minimum for the survival and flourishing of life anywhere.

Life

This is a basic value which is concomitant with the drive for self-preservation. "Life is in every aspect of the vitality which puts a human being in good shape for self-determination."[8] For the Igbo, *ndubuokwu,* means that life is a word; there must be life before all other things. Life is the condition for the possibility of what there is in terms of our humanity.

The realization of this basic human purpose requires, for its viability, a system of law. Accordingly, for Finnis, all human societies appear to show a significant measure of concern for the value of life; none allows killing without a fairly definite justification.

Knowledge

This is knowledge for its own sake rather than knowledge in pursuit of some other objective. It is driven by that primal human desire to know. It is driven by curiosity and ranges from pre-scientific to scientific, to mundane concerns and questions.

Knowledge that does not lead to truth as its end product is not worth pursuing. The principle that knowledge is in itself a good to be pursued, is for Finnis, self-evident and its value as a support and guide to action is not in need of further justification.

Play

This is a large and irreducible element in human culture. It involves "the engagement in performances which have no point beyond the

---

[8] J. Finnis, *Natural Law and Natural Rights,* Oxford: Clarendon, 1992, p. 190.

performance itself, enjoyed for its own sake."[9]

Aesthetic experience

This does not necessarily involve personal action. It is the inner experience involved in the appreciation of beauty in all its forms.

Sociability

In its broadest terms, this involves friendship. To be in friendship with other human kins is a fundamental form of human good. There is need for friendship for its own sake as well as in pursuit of other human objectives.

Practical reasonableness

We need practical reason to decide on life-style, moulding character and in the effective solution to problems consequent on the choices we make or fail to make.

Religion

Every culture recognizes an order of things "beyond each and every man." Without this, life may be a gaping void.

While justice and liberty are not listed as part of Finnis' seven irreducible human goods, both are presupposed. They clearly pervade and encompass the institutional framework intended to protect the human good. In the words of Grisez,

> "justice requires due respect for liberty which, while itself not one of the basic human goods, is a necessary condition for the active, human realization of any of those goods."[10]

Justice itself cannot be realized outside a system of law and its

---

[9] Ibid., p. 195.

[10] M. Grisez, *Life and Death with Liberty and Justice,* London: Butterworths, 1979, p. 180.

institutions. It is a system in which law is a vital aspect of man's culture and social existence; embodying the collective will of the community and binding the members of that community in a unity of purpose. In all of these, the exercise of reason is essential and indispensable.

In the face of the colonial and neo-colonial assumption of the non-existence of law, the evidence on the ground suggests something totally different. If anything, that evidence shows that: (a) the assumption was an essential part of the ideology of colonialism; (b) it was an important psychological armour which, in conjunction with the Bible and gunpowder, helped to bring about the physical, political, economic, and mental domination of non-Europeans.

The assumption becomes untenable once the following questions are posed:

(a) did these savage primitive people ever quarrel?;
(b) did they reason at all like other humans?;
(c) did they ever argue on any issue, or on issues concerning rights and entitlements; and
(d) if they quarrelled at all, how did they resolve disputes?

Once we begin to inquire into the kind of arguments and reasonings employed in the resolution of disputes among a people, we are confronted, not with a pseudo-legal or moral problem, but with one which, in itself, is complex and multifaceted.

Dispute settlement studies produced by legal anthropology provided me with an analytical framework. The works by Gluckman,[11] Fellers,[12] Bohannan,[13] and others are classics and pioneer studies but they are deficient in that not much attention was paid to the notion of justice. These works, in general, gave only scant attention to the norm of justice and to the structure of legal reasoning and argumentation. The only exception is Okafor.[14] Okafor made an effort to examine and explain justice in the broad framework of his analysis. But like the others before him, justice did not occupy a central position in his work.

Indeed, the analysis of legal rhetoric has been left to ethnographers

---

[11] Max Gluckman, *The Judicial Process Among The Barotse in Northern Rhodesia,* Manchester: University Press, 1955.

[12] Lloyd Fellers, *Law Without Precedents: Legal Ideas in Action in the Court of Colonial Basoga,* Chicago: University Press, 1969.

[13] Paul Bohannan, *Justice and Judgement Among the Tiv,* London: Oxford University Press, 1957.

[14] F.U. Okafor, *Igbo Philosophy of Law,* Enugu: Fourth Dimension, 1992.

and anthropologists who have often, but not always, ignored the context in which legal discourse operates. Underlying the mechanism of legal discourse is the quest for justice which, in Igbo studies,[15] has not been properly accounted for. As a consequence, a fruitful line of research has remained unexplored.

In this book, an attempt is made to elucidate the logical features of some fundamental concepts and phrases related to justice, dispute settlement, and the organization of life and work in Igbo communities in Aniocha north local government area of Delta State.

According to them, justice is a concept that permeates the whole social fabric. I admit that no Igbo community is unique in this respect because there is no human society or community where justice does not occupy a central position in terms of constituting the ultimate measure for the conduct of affairs at individual and community levels.

Otakpor has argued that "there is no society without a sense of justice, nor is there a society that is absolutely just or unjust, or a society that is beyond justice, that is, a society where there is no sense of justice."[16]

Yet in each human group there may be some marked and observed differences in terms of what constitutes a just desert or entitlement. While this is conceded, it should not be taken as an explicit endorsement of the view that justice is relative to culture or environment.[17]

This view is difficult to sustain because there are certain invariant norms shared by the human family. Most relevant is that our common physio-biological make up is definitive and universally shared. Furthermore, it is not difficult to discover that justice, law and order are universal, essential characters which belong to all human societies, primitive or modern, developed, under-developed or undeveloped, in the past, present and future.

This research work, including the interviews and data, has been restricted to a local government area in Delta State, which is (a) ethnically homogeneous, and (b) geographically contiguous, and this helps to establish ties and cleavages.

No generalizations are made from the data that is available. No sweeping claims are presented arising from the interviews and data. It is

---

[15] I am not aware of any text that has specifically dealt with justice among the Igbo in general or in a particular geographical setting.

[16] Nkeonye Otakpor, "A Sense of Justice," *Readings in Social and Political Philosophy*, Vol. 2, F.A. Adeigbo, ed., Ibadan: Claverianum Press, 1994, p. 32.

[17] Ibid., pp. 17-35

clear, however, that the Igbo of Aniocha north in Delta State is an integral part of the larger Igbo nation.

Even though the Igbo in the area under reference may be the *writ small* in the socio-cultural, political and economic configuration of the Igbo nation, it is possible that my conclusions are applicable to other Igbo communities. It is possible that other Igbo communities are affected by my thesis and conclusions.

Chapter 2

The Igbo in Aniocha north local government area

The people

Aniocha north local government area[1] was until recently, an integral part of Aniocha local government with its headquarters at Ogwashi-Ukwu. It was in the early 1990s that the local government at Ogwashi-Ukwu was split into two: Aniocha north and south with administrative headquarters located at Issele-Ukwu and Ogwashi-Ukwu respectively.

Aniocha north and south, and their siblings in Oshimili north and south, Ika north and south, Ndokwa east and west, and Ukwuani is home to the bulk of the Igbo, west of the River Niger. With minor differences the people in these areas speak one form of Igbo dialect or another. They speak the same language of related dialects which are mutually intelligible. The Igbo in these areas, particularly in Aniocha area, share a common culture, world view and normative order.

Aniocha north local government area is made up of three clans: Ezechima, Odiani and Idumuje.Ezechima include Issele-Ukwu, Issele-

---

[1] The area under reference was part of the defunct Western Region, part of the defunct Mid-West State upon creation in 1963, then the defunct Bendel and now part of Delta State.

Oshimili, Aniocha, and Ika were formally one – Asaba Division in the defunct Benin Province. Ndokwa and Ukwuani were then in Warri Division in the defunct Delta Province.

Aniocha and Oshimili areas are often referred to as Enuani. This is no more current. Anioma is the current use and embraces not only Aniocha and Oshimili but also Ika, Ndokwa, and Ukwuani.

Azagba, Issele-Mkpitime, Onitsha-Ukwu, Onitsha-Olona, Obior, Onitsha-Ugbo, Ezi and Obomkpa. It is on record that Onitsha in Anambra State claims Ezechima origin. Odiani clan includes Ugbodu, Ukwu-Nzu, Ugboba, Ubulubu and Idumu-Ogo. Idumuje clan is made up of Idumuje-Unor, Idumuje-Ugboko, and Aniofu.

In Odiani clan, there is another distinguishing factor. This is to be found in the Yoruba dialect *(Onugwumi)* which is spoken in Ugbodu, Ukwu-Nzu, Idumu-Ogo and two quarters in Ubulubu. The people in these areas also speak the Igbo dialect that is common to them.

According to their oral history, the people of Ugbodu, Ukwu-Nzu, and Idumu-Ogo trace their origin to Owo in Ondo State. Most of the people in Ezechima clan, on the other hand, following their oral history, trace their origin to Benin.

In spite of these divergent sources of origin, the Igbo of Aniocha North have over centuries of contact among themselves and with others, gradually developed (evolved) a commonality of perspectives in many things: language, marriage, burial rites of passage, birth ceremonies, proverbs, anecdotes, morality, and moral norms, the other world the reward system, customary jurisprudence and judicial procedure. Far more important, is the justice system that evolved over centuries of living, sharing and dying together.

In all the towns and villages except one – Ubulubu, the political system is, with minor differences, basically the same. In Ubulubu, the eldest *okpala* title holder is the *obi. Obi*ship thus moves from one person to the other, depending on who is older in terms of when the *okpala* title was taken.

In the other towns and villages, kingship *(obiship)* is hereditary and is based strictly on the rule of primogeniture. They are not divine kings though inherent in their office is the political, legal, religious and moral authority of their communities. Yet, it is a classic example of a system where the *obis* have neither power nor authority in an absolute sense. They are not as powerful as an *oba* in Yorubaland or as the *Oba* of Benin.

An *obi* is an *obi* by the grace of his people. The *obi* is a leader not a ruler. His primary function as the foremost public officer of his people is to represent them well, to direct cooperative activities of different sorts, to bind together members of his community. He has neither legislative, judicial nor executive functions. Consequently, he can neither compel personal obedience nor punish wrongdoers, except through *Izu Ani,* that is, the Council chaired by him.

World view

The Igbo, like other human groups, have a world view. The fact of our shared humanity validates this claim. What is a worldview? It is a general view of the universe and man's relationship to it. It is how the world is perceived, contemplated, intuited, conceived by people who live in it. This is expressed in their attitudes and belief systems. Let us examine the views of two other scholars.

For Ifesieh, it is,

> "a body of beliefs about the universe which are common among members of any society and existentially demonstrated in their value systems, such as their philosophy of life, social conduct and morality, folklores, myths, rites and rituals, norms, ideas, cognitive mappings and theologies."[2]

Metuh, on the other hand, suggests that worldview is,

> "the complex of a people's belief and attitudes concerning the origin, the nature, structure, organization, and interaction of beings in the universe with particular reference to man."[3]

For Ifesieh and Metuh, there is a multiplicity of beings. Besides, there are conceptual schemes, belief systems, common attitudes which are part of a people's worldview. These elements are not independent of each other. They interact and are intrinsically connected to each other.

Igbo world view

There is a general agreement, almost, among Igbo scholars on the basic structure of Igbo worldview. It is about how the Igbo, as a people, conceive, intuit, perceive, and contemplate the world. It is about Igbo belief systems, conceptual schemes, common attitudes, their

---

[2] E. I. Ifesieh, *Religion at the Grassroots: Studies in Igbo Religion,* Enugu, 1989, p. 20.

[3] E. I. Metuh, *Comparative Studies of African Traditional Religion,* Onitsha: Imico, 1987, p. 61.

philosophy, religion, theology, etc. This world view is the sole
determinant of their way of life. It provides explanation for reality,
materially and spiritually.

The Igbo worldview is fundamentally dualistic. Reality for them is
explicable in dual terms. So is the world and all there is. This dualism is
expressed in different ways: matter and spirit; visible and invisible; body
and spirit; material and immaterial.

The world itself is a composite of material and immaterial aspects.
That is to say that there are two realms or orders or spheres of existence.

a) *Ani-Mmadu:* This is the human world, *uwa,* the material world, of
   bodily things and the visible order.
b) *Ani Mmuo:* This is the spirit world, the immaterial world, the world
   of invisible order. This is the world of our ancestors and
   supernatural forces.

A human being known as *mmadu* is a composite of material body,
ahu, and spirit, *mmuo.* It is the combination of the body and spirit that
make a human being. Human beings are the main, prominent
inhabitants of *uwa,* hence *ani mmadu* or *uwa anyi no.*

The two worlds are necessarily interdependent. They are not
mutually exclusive because they overlap. The inhabitants of the two
worlds interact just as the two worlds intersect and overlap. There exists
a constant interaction between the two realms of existence. Similarly,
there exists a constant interaction between the two ineluctable aspects
of a human being. One without the other is chaos, real chaos
particularly in the visible, material world.

Otakpor has suggested that both worlds are conflated in the Igbo
order of knowledge taken as intuitive and as a general intellectual
configuration. Furthermore, he argues that:

> "the earth plane (this world) and the spiritual plane are
> coterminous. They exist side by side and none makes sense
> without the other. Yet the location of the spiritual plane
> which is beyond the earth plane is unknown."[4]

The spiritual plane is referred to as the beyond, that is, beyond the

---

[4] Nkeonye Otakpor, *"Onye Ma Ebe Ono?* (Who Knows Where He is?), *The Third Way in
African Philosophy: Essays in Honour of Kwasi Wiredu,* Olusegun Oladipo, ed.,
Ibadan: Hope, 2002, p. 146.

world of matter and also beyond the intellect and comprehension of human beings. However, the spirits are believed to be involved in the day to day affairs of human beings.

There is a hierarchy of beings as well as a multiplicity of beings, according to the Igbo. This multiplicity of beings is not a recipe for chaos. The universe is not in a disordered form because at the apex of the hierarchy is *Chi-ukwu* (God), and God is infinite order. In the Igbo pantheon, unlike the Greek one, the relationship between the gods is cordial and reciprocal. This ensures harmony at all levels of existence.

Chi-ukwu, as the creator of both worlds, is at the apex of the hierarchy of beings with dominion over the visible and invisible realms. God is spirit in its absoluteness and exercises absolute control over all there is. Yet, God is not closely involved in human affairs as such. The local deities and ancestral spirits are in charge acting as intermediaries between human beings and God. The deities and ancestral spirits control natural phenomena while God exercises overall superintending powers of creation, life and death.

The import of this should not be easily lost. Among the Igbo, God is not worshipped directly. God is worshipped indirectly through the local deities and ancestral spirits who function as the intermediaries. This is perhaps the only reason why there are no shrines dedicated to the worship of God in Igbo communities. The greatness and the mystery of God are diluted and desecrated in man-made shrines and grooves.

God is the final *arbiter* in the worldly affairs of human beings. Hence in the event of injustice, unfairness, etc., appeals from those dissatisfied with the judgment of men are made to God through the deities and ancestral spirits. Since God is infinite knowledge, *Chi ukwu ma,* and wisdom, a case before God goes nowhere else. It is at a dead end in the immaterial realm.

The justice of God, the Igbo believe, is not at all blind or mechanistic. It needs no courts of equity to redress imperfect and crooked judgments. The reason is that for them God is infinite equity, infinite and absolute justice.

Distribution of authority and power

Authority and power in these communities are divergent. Authority lies in the assembly of all adult citizens where major decisions concerning what and how they ought to be or how and what things ought to be are debated and taken. Power is exercised through the *Obi-in-Council* (the

Council).

The Council, chaired by the *obi*, is composed of all adult males who have taken the *okpala* title, elders who are neither title holders nor chiefs, and all other adult males. Apart from the *omu* who is a member by virtue of her position, women are excluded. Anybody who thinks that he has a contribution to make on any issue, can attend and take part in the proceedings of the Council. In principle, no member of the community is barred from attending meetings in the palace unless those under one form of punishment or the other.

The Council is equivalent to a house of assembly or representatives but with these differences: there is never an election because every adult represents himself or herself always, as well as his/her lineage. It is the highest judicial body. It is the court of first and last instance. It reviews cases sent to it from the lower bodies, organs, associations, lineages and age-groups. It is therefore, the court of last resort in customary matters. Where the need arises it can review its own decisions. Before the advent of colonialism, it dealt with civil and criminal matters. Now it has jurisdiction only on civil matters. The current judicial opinion is not antithetic to this. "It is well settled and judicial authority is not lacking for the view that persons exercising judicial functions in accordance with native law and custom... have always been recognized as having such powers. The provisions of the Constitution of 1979, Sections 6(1) and (5) have not altered this judicial position."[5]

By implementing decisions taken by itself or those passed on to it by the assembly of adult citizens, the Council functions as an executive. It follows that the legislative, executive, and judicial powers are fused into one: the Council. There is no explicit differentiation between politics, law, morality and justice. These are fused in the dynamics of Igbo culture and tradition.

Roles are differentiated, at all levels. While power is widely diffused in political and legal domains. Legal and political roles are necessarily conflated because of the primary desire of the communities in using power to maintain law and order.

The system of ranking is strictly observed in sitting arrangements, in sharing kolanuts, wine and food, yet this system is not rigid. Recruitment of members of the Council is not based on any hereditary principle. Wealth, age, and pedigree are not the only important indices, though they count.

Individuals of lowly status may become not just members, but

---

[5] *Agu* v. *Ikevribe*, (1991) 3 NWLR, p. 385. This was restated in *Ohiaeri* v. *Akabezi*, (1992) 2 NWLR, I.

influential members through ability shown in public debate. Among the qualities highly esteemed in this regard are bravery in war, good farming skills, skill in debate, soundness of argument, and knowledge of customary law and precedents. Men who combine some of these qualities with a passion for truth and demonstrated loyalty to community affairs are usually sought for in the resolution of disputes, private and public.

The Council has an inner cabinet in most towns and villages, composed of the *obi* and the most senior chiefs. But whatever they do or say, they are careful not to appear to be imposing their own decisions or versions of reality on a community whose public space is always indeterminate, and has the virtue of belonging to no one in particular. Just as no one can be barred from this public space, so no one can appropriate, colonize or harvest it for private and selfish ends.

The public space, in most Igbo communities in which the question, what and how we ought to be, is debated has the virtue of belonging to no one. Therefore, no one particular individual (rank, status, birth, notwith-standing) can claim to determine its limits. The unique feature of this space is that it is avowedly republican. It is a public space in which multiplicities of voices celebrate their presence. It is a space that is beyond any particular determination that might capture it and thereby predetermine what ought to be without need of deliberation.

This republican public space where debates concerning what and how the Igbo ought to be is essentially necessary in terms of Igbo passion for justice. One proverb affirms that when a decision is taken or a judgement is given in a room with the doors and windows firmly locked, that decision or judgement will become public when the doors and windows are opened.

The public space is equivalent to an Igbo court of wisdom where all well informed citizens evaluate alternatives and reach considered judgements about basic political, moral and judicial concerns. In this court, the Igbo look at all sides of a question, proposition or claim before they reach a decision. For the Igbo, like other humans, wisdom comes with experience, and that is the product of a long life. But because the capacity for practical wisdom can be found among young people, some of whom seem to have a natural inclination to make the right decisions and choices, no voice is excluded or silenced in this court.

There is no centralization of political power and authority but this does not mean the absence of government. Centralization is not the only *sine qua non* of government. The absence of a central authority also means that sovereign power does not inhere in any one person, a group of persons, a family or group of families. Among the Igbo of the area under reference it is no political slogan to affirm that sovereignty belongs to the people. This is the reality on the ground.

The basic social unit is the single village consisting of several families linked together by ties of kinship. They share the same cultural identity, guardian deity, and the most important cultural symbol: *ofo. ofo* is also the symbol of religious and political authority and power within the small family group, as well as the extended family group.

Ofo, apart from its religious, political and cultural relevance, is also an instrument of justice. Nwala has suggested that,

> "the highest principle which is the corner-stone of the behaviour and actions among all being is justice, symbolized in *Ofo* which is held by the elders, priests and the initiated. In the realm of human intercourse this cosmic and social order is crystallized in *Omenani.*"[6]

It is believed that the holder of *ofo* is endowed with spiritual powers by the ancestors and the gods. In some communities, it is the symbol of authority for the eldest male member of the family, that is, *di okpala.* By virtue of this, he is the spiritual as well as the political head of the family.

At his level, he also holds court, in which he exercises judicial powers and functions, with other senior male members of the family. He holds the family land, assets and liabilities in trust and must always ensure that members receive their due.

For a member of the community to assert: *E ji m ofo* or *ofo ka mji,* means proclaiming innocence before the ancestors and the gods. *E ji m ofo* is a categorical proclamation of innocence before the community, the ancestral spirits and the gods. This proclamation is a frontal embrace of truth before men, spirits and the gods.

For this reason the keeper of *ofo* must be fair to all, honest, just, objective, unprejudiced and morally impeccable. Like Ceaser's wife, he must be above board.

Ofo is, thus, not merely a status symbol, a religious and political symbol; it is also, and most important, a judicial symbol. It is a most powerful judicial instrument. Its use, its presence in any adjudicatory situation ensures that litigants, witnesses, the audience must be fair and just in their dealings.

---

[6] T. U. Nwala, *Igbo Philosophy,* Lagos: Lantern Books, 1985, p. 58.

Nwala further explains that,

> *"Ofo* is a legal instrument for validating decisions of the family lineage, village or clan. It helps to ensure political stability by its role as a means of sanction, settling disputes, and ensuring peace, harmony and conformity. It expresses the will of the community including the living and the dead ancestors and the gods."[7]

Ofo, as the symbol of justice and morality is a binding force. It binds the community together. It binds men, spirits and gods together and serves as an instrument of cosmic and social order.

In an adjudicatory situation, especially one that has proved difficult to settle because of the intransigence, lack of cooperation or arrogance on the part of a party to a dispute, the *ofo* holder can ask the party in question to swear to *ofo.* Here, *ofo* is used to enforce compliance and conformity, elicit truth and punish those who engage in deliberate falsehood.

Finally, for *ofo* holders and elders who work closely with them, all walk a tight rope, trying to maintain the demands of fairness and justice, harmony and order, the spiritual and profane. In walking this tight rope, they must ensure that truth is their watchword, because sickness and/or death is the penalty for infractions on their part.

In spite of the plurality of social and political units, the Igbo in Aniocha North, whether Ezechima, Odiani or Idumuje, are one subculture. They are geographically contiguous. The religious order affirms *Chi-ukwu* (God) as the origin of all there is. *Chi-ukwu* is the beginning and end of all things. They share a common way of life because the culture is the same.

Mechanisms for integration

They operate some integrating mechanisms like the existence of some powerful deities or oracles. For example, there is the *Mkpitime* among the Ezechima, particularly the inhabitants of Issele-Ukwu, Issele-Azagba, and Issele-Mkpitime. There is the *Nnemonicha* among the Idumuje clan which is located at Idumuje-Uno, and the *Onitcha-Kodi* located at Ukwu-Nzu which is prominent among the Odiani. In each

---

[7] Ibid., p. 65

village or town there are oracles *(Iyi)* and deities which function as potent reinforcing mechanisms.

The prevalence of markets and market days with the same name is another powerful reinforcing mechanism. In the whole area, there are four-day honoured market days: *Olie, Afor, Nkwo,* and *Eke.* Before the advent of colonialism, *Eke* was (still so regarded) the "native" Sunday – a day set aside for worship, meetings and rest. These market days have another important function – they are used in the recording of time and events in the community.

Each town or village has a market day. Market days are focal points for all the people in the area. The largest of these markets held every four days are: *Olie* at Onitsha-Olona, *Nkwo* at Idumuje-Unor and *Afor* at Issele-Ukwu. Of all these markets the most prominent among them is *Afor* held at Issele-Ukwu. The entire Aniocha North is at a stand still on this market day because many people are attracted there. Apart from the normal transactions for which markets are known, these markets are also social centres where social engagements take place.

The rule of exogamy is another reinforcing mechanism. The practice of exogamy has helped form an intricate network of relationships integrating personal, the familial and the village group. In such marriages persons and families in a village group are inexorably linked to other persons and families in another village group. The two village groups are also linked as a result of this. The reason for this is obvious: marriage involves, but transcends, the two individuals concerned, because it is an affair that involves two families or village groups or both. Therefore, "beneath the apparent fragmentation of authority lay deep fundamental unities not only in the religious and cultural spheres, but also in matters of politics and economics."[8] The justice system is not excluded from these deep fundamental unities.

Parallel to the multiplicity of social and political units is the multiplicity of legal skills. Just as there is no central political authority yet there is government, so there is no central judicial authority yet there is no absence of law and order. There is a system of justice even in the absence of a central judicial authority. There are no legal institutions but laws are made and offenders against law and order and custom are punished. There is an excess of legal skills just as there is an excess of democracy.

The reason for this is not far to seek. Elders, family and quarter heads exercise judicial functions out of the framework of customary law

---

[8] Kenneth Onwuka Dike, *Trade and Politics in the Niger Delta 1830–1885*, Oxford: Clarendon Press, 1956, p. 44.

and practice.[9] It is well accepted that one of the many ways of settling disputes in Igbo (perhaps in many other groups in Nigeria) is to refer the matter to a family head or an elder or group of elders for resolution.

For such a resolution to be effective, credible and binding, it must be based on the subsequent acceptance by both parties. This is why the view that dispute settlement in most indigenous communities is through consensus, mediation and compromise, has been vigorously advanced.

In the Igbo idea of litigation, therefore, the elders endeavour to look far beyond the respective claims of the parties to the dispute. They try to examine the relationship which is extant, and which is likely to prevail between the parties after the adjudicatory process. The underlying idea is the emphasis laid on the fact that no party should be overly encouraged to celebrate victory, because there is neither victor nor vanquished, winner nor loser in a quarrel between and among brothers and sisters.

Methods of dispute resolution

There are many methods of dispute resolution. While some of these methods are found in Igbo culture, some are not. Diagrams 1 and 2 are graphic presentations of these methods, (see pp. 32 and 33).

Self help

This means that the victim of any wrongdoing can on his/her own seek redress in order to assuage the wrong done. Information gathered from fieldwork showed that self help as a method of dispute resolution has never been part of Igbo lifestyle. Blood feuds were never employed as a mechanism for dispute settlement. The idea that individuals should act on their own, amounts to seeking revenge. There is no encouragement for anyone who seeks revenge, (see diagram 2, p.33).

---

[9] George Elombi, "Customary Arbitration: A Ghanaian Trend Reversed in Nigeria," *African Journal of International and Comparative Law* (AJICL), Vol. 5, No. 4, 1993, p. 807.

Assembly of peer group members

The best example of this is *Izu Omu,* an association or group of women and some men usually headed by the *Omu.*

There are offences that are peculiar to women or involve the womenfolk alone. Such offences are in the first instance looked into by women's groups, for example, the *Omu* association or *Otu Inwene,* another peer group assembly of women only.

The basic idea is that members of a peer group are better equipped in terms of understanding the issues in which members are involved. This idea is reinforced when those involved in a dispute are both members of the same peer group.

If the peer group assembly is unable to resolve the problem, it is referred to the *Obi-in-council* for final determination.

Family meeting

This is known as *Izu Ebo,* a meeting of all adult male members of a lineage. Old female members are allowed to participate. So are old women who are members of the family by marriage.

This meeting has the responsibility of settling disputes between members as well as between them and non-members. The meeting is headed by the most senior adult male whose symbol of authority is the *ofo.* He has moral, political and religious authority over his kith and kin. He mediates between the living and the dead members of the group.

In cases of dispute, the usual settlement mechanisms are employed *(see chapter four).* Those dissatisfied appeal to the village meeting.

Village meeting

This is known as the *izu ogbe.* The assembly comprises all adult male citizens; women are excluded so are young persons in their teens. The assembly functions as a legislative body for the purpose of enacting laws, the strengthening of existing ones or their clarification. It also functions as a judicial assembly where conflicts are resolved. Appeals by those dissatisfied with its decisions are taken to the *Obi-*in-council.

The Obi-in-Council

This body has been discussed earlier in this chapter.

Secret societies

It was found that unlike in other pre-colonial and post-colonial societies in Nigeria, there were never secret societies among the Igbo in Aniocha area. There is nothing comparable with or equivalent to the *Ogboni* among the Yoruba or the *Ekpe* secret society among the Efik.

Matters dealt with in both the Village meeting and the Council are normally those of common concern to all members of the community. These are common problems, for which collective action or intervention was required, conflicts which threatened the cohesiveness of the community, for example, a dispute between members of different lineages, and a dispute between one community and another.

Both institutions always dealt with public policy issues publicly. Furthermore, the Council has the additional responsibility of relations between its own community and others.

To summarise, the resolution of disputes takes different forms depending on the origin of a dispute, the relationship between the parties to the dispute and the subject matter of the dispute. The mode of discourse is that of proverb, parable and metaphor, all drawn from the body of Igbo tradition.

Legal as well as political knowledge is accessible to all Igbo, reared and nurtured by, and with proverbs, parables and metaphor. Influential speeches imply the creative and skilful use of this tradition to provide counsel, elicit sympathy, justification and gradually nudge consensus.

Be that as it may, decisions are made after settlement through one or the combination of these:

1. family meetings and lineage assemblies;
2. assembly of all adults excluding women;
3. women's meetings and assembly where some men are participants *(Izu Inwene);*
4. age grades;
5. professional associations;
6. funeral meetings and ceremonies;
7. markets;
8. annual festivals and rituals;

9.   oracles and diviners;
10.   *Obi*-in-council.

Methods of dispute resolution

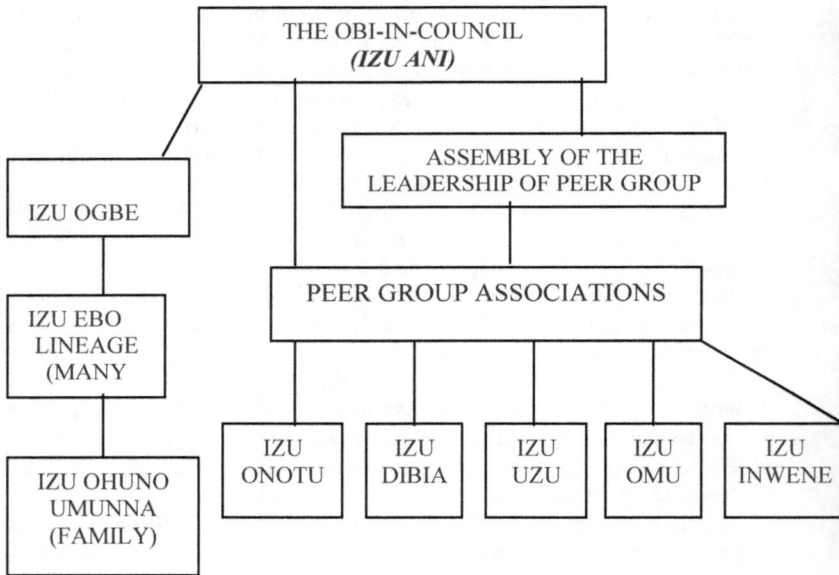

Diagram 1

Methods of institutionalizing legal action

Action in breach of Igbo norms →	Counteraction →	Correction
Norms, rules, principles and conventions at the background of events	*Kinds of counteraction*	*Restitution*
	(a) Self-help	(a) Not part of the Igbo justice system.
	(b) Contest or ordeal.	(b) Not part of the Igbo justice system
	(c) Family, lineage, village and town meetings.	
	(d) Professional and non-professional associations.	(c) Fines, reparative sanctions and open apologies through the town crier.
	(e) Obi-in-council.	(d) Ditto.
		(e) Ditto.

*Adapted with modifications from Paul Bohannan, *Social Anthropology,* New York: Holt and Rinehart, 1963, p. 296.

Diagram 2

Chapter 3

The root idea of justice in Igbo

The sense of justice is innate and universal

All human beings have a sense of justice. There is no human group
without a sense of justice. It is true that human beings are born with
neither vice nor virtue, that is, without a sense of wrong or right. The
socialization process is intended to teach this as well as other social
norms regarded as imperatives for the survival, good, and order of
society.

Yet it does not necessarily follow that a sense of justice is inclusive
of the norms, rules, regulations, and maxims of society to be taught as
part of the socialization process. A sense of justice and injustice is
innate. It is as innate as a sense of hunger, laughter, anger or sex.

The socialization process does not include coitus just as it does not
include a sense of justice and injustice. Coitus, crying, laughing,
humour, hunger, pain and pleasure are all innate.

It is absurd to suggest that a new born baby has to be taught how to
cry and how to smile. No one does the teaching and no one has been
taught. This is applicable to other human activities that are innate.
Nature, if anything, is the best teacher in respect of these activities.

In the same vein, a sense of justice and injustice is not taught to any
one. Since it is innate, it follows that it is neither given nor received
from or by anybody. It is neither received knowledge nor wisdom. It is a
gift from nature. A sense of revulsion against injustice is natural and
universal.[1]

---

[1] For a discussion of the universality of a sense of justice see Nkeonye Otakpor, "A sense
of Justice," *op. cit.,* pp. 17-35. See also Agnes Heller, *Beyond Justice,* Oxford:

Igbo culture and tradition

Tradition means opinions, beliefs, and customs handed down from generation to generation. These opinions, beliefs and customs constitute the patterns of thought and action which have been inherited. These may be in respect of religious, political, judicial or social thought and practice.

It involves cultural continuity in attitudes and institutions that sustain them. The Igbo tradition is embodied in one word: *Omenani.*[2] *Omenani* means all that is accepted in an Igbo community in terms of thought and action. To speak and act, that is, to live in accordance with the dictates of *Omenani* is to live according to what an Igbo community accepts in terms of its dominant ethos, norms, conventions, rules and regulations.

Omenani

Apart from the Igbo east of the Niger who wrote the undecoded *Nsibidi,* the Igbo in Aniocha have no written records of their pre-colonial past. This is not peculiar to them. Most traditional societies in Africa and elsewhere have no such records. From this, it cannot be concluded that such people have no past, no culture and tradition, no religion and philosophy, no morality and law.

To trace the processes of Igbo religion, philosophy and life style in general is a difficult enterprise, especially in the absence of written records. It may be difficult but not impossible. All that has been preserved of the Igbo myths, religion, philosophy, songs, literature, etc., have come down to us from one generation to another by word of mouth. Together, these form what the Igbo regard as *Omenani.*

Oge Enu Gbo, for short, *Oge gbo* or *Enu gbo* or *Oge mbu,* that is, the time past, the time of the ancestors *(in diebus illis)* is the starting point of *Omenani.* It is often directly associated with the ancestors who it is said received laws and morality from God *(Chi ukwu)* which they then passed on to their descendants in the form of customs and

---

Blackwell, 1987, pp. 1-47.

[2] Other words with equivalent meaning are *Odinani, Odibendi, and Omenala.* Apart from *Omenani* there is also *Amami ife ndi Igbo-Igbo wisdom,* and *Akiko Uwa* – Igbo folklore.

traditions. Hence *Omenani* is a cluster concept which embraces Igbo laws, principles, customs, traditions, morality and way of life. It is static and has supernatural sanction.

Omenani, therefore, means that which is done in the land or what obtains in the land. It is a generic term for the body of Igbo socio-religious laws, customs and tradition, etc., passing from one generation to another and having its origin as far back as from the time of the ancestors.

Omenani is a tradition in terms of its being handed down from generation to generation. On this account it is dynamic. It is a custom because it is the embodiment of accepted practices. This exemplifies its static aspect. These distinctions are, however, academic in the world of those whose lives are shaped by *Omenani.*

As a custom, *Omenani* is sacred. To that extent, it transcends the profane. And to the extent of its sacredness it is unchangeable. It is not subject to the vagaries of life in terms of its requirements and demands. It is closely linked with the earth goddess or spirit, hence it is revered and respected.

It is in the light of these that Ilogu argued that,

> "*Omenani* is derived from the goddess of *Ala (Ani)* and sanctioned by the ancestors, it is religious in nature, although it fulfils social, moral and cultural functions. It's hold on the community derives from the power of the goddess and the ancestors. Hence the unquestioned obedience which the community gives to it."[3]

It follows that *Omenani* has a metaphysical foundation and serves to validate or invalidate acts or omissions in all aspects of life. No breaches of it go unpunished. It is the sole means by which an Igbo community enforces conformity and justice. Hence for P. Iroegbu,[4] *Omenani* is the constitution or the legal code of the Igbo. Ilogu further explains that,

> "No breach of *Omenani* goes unpunished. Tradition prescribes the various things that must be done to take away the evil effects of such breaches or else the spirit of the ancestors and *Ani* will plague the society. *Omenani* therefore

---

[3] Edmund Ilogu, *Christianity and Igbo Culture,* New York: NOK, 1974, p. 23.

[4] Panthaleon Iroegbu, *The Kpin of Politics,* Owerri: International Press, 1996, p. 25.

becomes the means by which traditional Igbo society
ensures conformity and justice."[5]

Omenani also induces as well as encourages an inductive outlook
towards life. For example, it is not uncommon for the Igbo to give as
reason for supporting or rejecting an act or omission as follows:

a) this "X" cannot be done because our ancestors never did it;
b) this was never heard of since the time of our ancestors;
c) this "X" will work because it worked for our ancestors;
d) the earth goddess sanctioned "X", so it cannot be otherwise;

This means that the past is always present and affects everything
that happens. It means that acts or omission are justified or not on the
basis of the past.

It is clear that for the Igbo, *Omenani* is the source of knowledge, "of
knowing anything at all of their theodicy, their theogony as well as their
cosmology. It gives a clue to what they thought and believed about
these, and their relationship to heaven and earth," to material and
immaterial aspects of nature, between man *qua* man, between man and
community.

It enables us to discern that the fundamental questions of life have
been asked and answered by the Igbo in their own way, and that it is in
consequence of these questions and answers that the body of *omenani*
now available to us has come to be.

Omenani regulates life and all there is in an Igbo community. It
functions as an all embracing regulatory mechanism governing all
aspects of life, work, leisure, marriage, birth, initiation, religion, burial
practices, law and morality.

Omenani is derived from a conjunction of two words: *ome* and *ani.*
"*Ome* means as it is done (3rd person, impersonal from *ime* meaning
"to do", to "happen", "to obtain)". *Omume* means conduct, deed,
righteousness. *Ome* and *omume* thus have the same etymological root
and reference.

Ani means land, soil, ground or earth. Hence, the reference to *ani* as
the earth goddess which is the goddess of fertility. *Ani* is the symbolic
and metaphysical representation of *Chi ukwu,* the great spirit, the
supreme, indivisible one. *Na* is a preposition and it means "in/on".

---

[5] Edmund Ilogu, *op. cit.,* p. 23.

According to Nwala,

> "*Omenani* is a community enterprise. It refers to Igbo attitude to life and their basic conceptions about nature, society and life. It embraces the whole system of civilization of the Igbo in theory and practice. It contains within itself the principles for propagating and protecting Igbo traditional way of life. Myths, rituals, initiation rites, education and the socialization of the young, and sanctions were the means of propagating and protecting traditional Igbo civilization."[6]

Omenani poignantly describes the Igbo way of life. It is linked with the sense of mystery, with the mythic dimension and the supernatural. The spirit of *Omenani* is for Edeh,

> "linked with the sense of mystery and the supernatural. The idea of making sure that all is in tune with the community of being which includes the sensory and the supra-sensory realities is always at the background of the thought and actions of the people, whether they are thinking and acting as a community or as individuals."[7]

There is a requirement of *Omenani* as it particularly pertains to individuals. It is the requirement of absolute conformity, submission and identification of the indivi-dual with the community. This implies compliance with the norms, rules and regulations of the community to which the individual belongs.

Individuated value systems are aberrant because *Oha ka madu* (public interests are to be preferred to private ones). This requirement does not mean the negation of selfhood and individual freedom. It does not mean the suppression of person-hood nor does it amount to disownness because Igbo community is not a Leviathan that oppresses the individual for the fun of it. In the words of Obiechina,

> "it would be wrong to interpret the concentration of common goods and the primacy of the common interest as a matter of suppression of the personality from the outside, or

---

[6] T.U. Nwala, *Igbo Philosophy,* Lagos: Lantern Books, 1985, p. 8.

[7] E.M.P. Edeh, *Towards an Igbo Metaphysics*, Chicago: Loyola University Press, 1985, p. 61.

constraint on the part of an authority. Social conformity and the discouragement of deviation are not the same thing as the repressive curbing of individual freedom. Social freedom is related to legality and this is expressed as the principle of the greatest good of the greatest number. Traditional social philosophy is based on this principle and because it is fundamental to the very survival and general health of the society, is given validity by being anchored in customary practice and protected by divine and ancestral authority."[8]

Omenani is, *ipso facto*, the reference point and a guide against deviation.[9] Actions, activities and statements are measured against the standards and precepts of *Omenani* in terms of their acceptance or rejection, or their being good or bad, moral or immoral. To act or say something against the precepts of *Omenani* is to act or say something outside the way of life of the community. Laws, morals, and justice are measured against the precepts of *Omenani* in terms of their acceptability or rejection.

Individuals who are deviant are not only against the precepts of *Omenani,* they are in a most profound sense against the public *(Oha)* and its interest. They are also pitching their tents against *Chi ukwu* (God), the ancestors and *Ani* – the earth goddess. According to Njaka,

"Law and order are maintained because the ancestors so desire and *Oha* so commands. And the ancestors desire law and order because *Chiukwu* must have approved them."[10]

From the foregoing, it is plain that *Omenani* embodies the precepts, principles and standards with which to evaluate individual and community life in an Igbo community. It prescribes how life is to be lived and how things can be done in order to maintain law, order, peace and good government. All these are directed at two supreme ends: (a) the protection of life and property, and (b) the maintenance, enhancement and protection of the conditions that make the flourishing of human life possible.

---

[8] E. Obiechina, *Culture, Tradition and Society in the West African Novel*, Cambridge: University Press, 1971. pp. 202-203.

[9] F.U. Okafor, *Igbo Philosophy of Law, op. cit*, p. 68.

[10] E.N. Njaka, *Igbo Political Culture*, Evanston: Northwestern University Press, 1974, p. 46.

Without *Omenani*, therefore, an Igbo community will be in chaos and may not be substantially different from the Hobbesian state of nature where life is "nasty, brutish and short" because there are no laws, no morality, no justice, and no government.

I have argued *(in chapter one)* that there has always been law in Igbo communities. These communities were never replicas of the Hobbesian state of nature. If it is the case that without *Omenani* these communities would degenerate into the state of nature, it follows that *Omenani* embodies all that is required to avoid the slide into that ignoble state; where law, morality, religion, politics, socialization, custom, etiquette, *etc.,* are totally absent.

Among the Igbo the word "law" has a two fold meaning: *Omenani* and law, that is, *Iwu: Iwu Obodo,* the laws enacted for the administration of a town. As Ifemesia has explained,

> "literally, *Omenani* means action in accordance with (the stipulations of) the land, while *iwu* means something decided, enacted or struck. *Odinani* (what inheres in the land) and *Odibendi* (what abides in a people's homeland), the synonyms closest to *Omenani* also emphasize the autochthonous and natural element in the concept of *Omenani,* in contrast to the acquired and artificial quality of *iwu, Omenani* is inextricably bound up with mother earth and her tenants, the ancestors, and so cannot be easily altered or repealed; whereas *iwu* is enacted by living man and can be revoked by living man. *Omenani,* or *Omenala,* or *Odinani* or *Odibendi* conveys the idea of customary law which no one can really make or strike."[11]

The difference is obvious. Laws are susceptible to change, revocation or amendment because they are man-made whereas *Omenani* is not because it is bound up with mother earth and the ancestors. Njaka has suggested that laws are put in place because the ancestors so decreed, and the former so desired because *Chi ukwu* (God) approved.

The confusion introduced by this subtle distinction by Ifemesia is rather unfortunate. Contrary to his claim, law as *iwu* or as *Omenani* is man-made. His explanation in respect of this distinction is not very clear. The difference between law as *Omenani* and as *iwu,* is unclear.

---

[11] Chieka Ifemesia, *Traditional Humane Living Among the Igbo: An Historical Perspective,* Enugu: Fourth Dimension 1980, p. 35.

Omenani embodies customary law.

In the light of this confusion, customary law will simply be understood here as an integral part of *Omenani.* The reason for this choice is obvious. Until the advent of colonial rule, customary law was the only kind of law that the Igbo knew and used. Besides, in Aniocha North, the area under reference, any law – *iwu obodo,* that is opposed to *Omenani* has no chance of survival. It will self-destruct because it cannot be accepted by the people. Such a law has no cultural home, lacks legitimacy, and is not credible, traditionally. That cultural home or base is *Omenani,* that credibility and legitimacy can only be provided by *Omenani.*

Omenani is a basic norm

According to Nwala, *Omenani* "contains within itself the principles for propagating and protecting Igbo traditional way of life." For Edeh, it is at "the background of the thought and actions of the people", while for Ifemesia "it conveys the idea of customary law". Okafor suggests that "it is the basic foundation".

Of these approaches, among the many others, only those of Okafor, Edeh and Nwala allude to something fundamental and profound concerning *Omenani.* It does not just contain within itself the principles underlying the traditional way of life of the Igbo, nor is it merely the background of the thought and actions of the people. *Omenani* is far more than these.

In itself, *Omenani* is a principle that is not derived from outside itself. It is not just the background to something or to everything; it is the ground without a back. It is its own ground or foundation as well as the ground or foundation for all there is among the Igbo. It is a basic principle, or, following Kelsen, it is the basic norm. It is basic because no questions can be raised concerning the basis of its validity. As a basic norm it provides the ground for the objective validity of Igbo thought and practice, or traditional way of life.

Norms are regulations stating in precise terms how people are to behave. Norms are standards, and so refer to the ought realm. Norms do not express what is, or what is done, or what must be the case, but what ought to be. They are valid because of their objective facticity. They exist, they are there. All other norms are dependent on the basic norm, but *ex hypothesis,* the basic norm does not rest upon other norms. It rests upon itself. It is its own foundation.

Omenani as a basic norm, *ex hypothesis,* does not originate from another norm, legal or moral. It is not the creation of any legal or moral mechanism. *Omenani* is a presupposition of socio-cultural and jural thought. It is "meta-legal" in Kelsenian terms. It is legal, if by that is meant anything which has legally relevant functions. *Omenani* is also meta-moral, for exactly the same reasons. It is moral, if by that is meant anything which has morally relevant functions. But *Omenani* is not a basic norm for legal and moral purposes only. It is as cultural, social, religious and political as it is legal and moral because it has relevant functions in these domains. *Omenani* is the only standard or reference point for all of these and more.

The derivation of justice

The idea of justice is to be extracted from Igbo culture and language. There is no single word in Igbo language which succinctly explains justice, like *jus* among the ancient Greeks and Romans.

Among the ancient Romans, *jus* has a variety of meanings in Roman Law. It could mean "a place where justice is dispensed *(Jus vocatio),* or strict law as distinct from equity, or a right deriving from a rule *(Jus conubii),* or general man-made law as opposed to *fas,* that is, law declared by divine authority. From the foregoing, *jus* came to have particularly important meanings: (a) the rules of law, and (b) the rights conferred by those rules on a person in particular situations."[12]

In the classical period, another term was coined, "*acquitas,* which meant fairness, justice, and was often used in reference to the Praetorian interpretation and application of the law."[13]

Jus as precepts of law were enumerated in the institutes. "It means to live honourable, not to hurt one another, to give each man his due. Ulpian, the Roman jurist defined justice as *suum cuique tribuere,* that is, the constant and perceptual wish to give each man his due."[14]

Unlike *Jus* justice in Igbo is derived from the conjunction of several words and phrases. As in ancient Roman times it has demonstrated conceptual as well as epistemological difficulties.

For example: The word "*olu*" means: "(a) work or talk (b) fault,

---

[12] L.B. Curson, *Roman Law,* London: MacDonald and Evans. 1966. p. 14.

[13] Ibid., p. 14.

[14] Ibid., p. 14.

weakness of behaviour in human beings."[15] From *olu* the following phrases are derived:

a) *"ife na olu:* prize or reward;
b) *Ugwo olu:* reward, payment for work down;
c) *Nee olu:* reward, payment for work down;
d) *Lu ajo olu:* to do some work badly, or to do bad work";[16]
e) *Onye olu oma:* the person who does good work;
f) *Onye ajo olu:* the person who does bad work.

Olu, which means work, refers to human endeavour in any sphere of human activity. It does not solely or specifically refer to manual work alone. The challenge of being human is in itself a work of a specific, special kind. There are bad and good human beings, moral and immoral ones, just as there are good and bad blacksmiths, carpenters, teachers, politicians, lawyers, native doctors and traditional birth attendants. This classification is not arbitrarily determined. It is hinged on an Igbo community's standards of judgement.

A work is good or bad in relation to community standards of judgement. These derivations from *olu,* therefore, have heavy accretions in Igbo morality, law and socio-cultural life in general. A work is judged to be bad not because of the person involved but because it fails to meet the acceptable standard as enshrined in *Omenani.* In some cases, a work is judged bad because of human weakness. The converse is the case.

The moral concepts denoting good and bad, or good and evil are *oma* and *njo. Njo* means "evil, badness, wickedness, sin".[17] From *njo* the following phrases are derived:

a) *"afo njo:* unkindness;
b) *jo njo:* be bad, wicked, evil, ugly, refusal to share, for example food;
c) *onye njo:* sinner, evil person, bad person, niggardly person."[18]

Oma means "good, fine, pleasing, nice or beautiful."[19] From *oma*

---

[15] Kay Williamson, *Igbo-English Dictionary*, Benin City: Ethiope Publishing, 1972, p. 418.
[16] Ibid., p. 418.
[17] Ibid., p. 310.
[18] Ibid., p. 310.
[19] Ibid., p. 419.

the following phrases are derived:

a) *afo oma:* kindness;
b) *ife oma:* a nice, good thing.
c) *Iru oma:* favour, goodness, good omen.
d) *Isi oma:* good luck; (this is a female name).
e) *nwe afo oma:* be generous, kind, benevolent.
f) *Onodu oma:* good condition.[20] (The good condition can be in mental, psychical, psychological or physical aspects).

From the derivations from *olu, njo* and *oma,* the norm of justice can be easily extracted, constructed and reconstructed. There is the strong belief in reward or payment for work done or not done. No one has an escape from reward for work done or not done, because no one is without reward for act or omission.

Olu onye ne che-e means that the reward for your work awaits you because *onye obuna ga ana ugwo olu – a.* No work done or undone is without its reward. Therefore, reward is available on either side of the coin in the phenomenal drama of life which is epitomized in the choices we make or fail to make.

The reward is not arbitrarily determined. It is, instead, measured and determined in relation to the work done or undone, the choices made or not made, the decisions taken or not. Your work, choice and decision solely determine your lot, due or reward. This is not much different from the saying that people reap what they sow. The nature and essence of work done or not done determine the extent and quality of reward.

Any person who escapes from getting reward for work done or undone here and now has a case to answer before the ancestors, *Ani* – the earth goddess and *Chi ukwu* (God). Some one may find an escape from getting reward from the community but there is no such escape from the ancestors, and from *Ani* and *Chi ukwu*. Like the Greeks who believed that no one has an escape from the Moira of their gods, so the Igbo believe that no one has an escape from the good or evil consequences of the work done or undone, the choices made or not made, the decisions taken or not taken.

Olu oma and *ajo olu* (good work and bad, evil work) are social acts. A social act is either in breach of a norm or is not. A norm, custom, ethical code or precept, etc. is not a social act. So, *Omenani* is not a

---

[20] Ibid., p. 419.

social act. A norm is a communally recognized and accepted guide to action. Breaches of a norm are social acts, and these breaches demand restitution and readjustment in order to restore the original balance, the prior social equilibrium which was disjointed by a social act. *Omenani* prescribes the sanction for breaches of Igbo norms, ethical codes, etc. It specifies the rights, duties and privileges conferred by those rules on a person in a particular situation.

Justice: the web of Igbo society

For the Igbo, justice is the web of society.[21] A spider's web is a complicated network of points. These points are independent. Yet they are so linked to each other that when one point is touched, the entire web is disturbed. The web reverberates. The several points structurally linked make a web what it is; they do not have meaning outside the web. It is within the structure of the web that meaning has to be sought.

The structure of the spider's web and its internal dynamics have some relevance for Igbo society, and perhaps, for all other societies and communities. The network of societal linkages is constituted primarily by individual Igbo persons who as members function in different capacities within society. Justice constitutes the unseen thread which ties two things simultaneously: (a) ties together all the individuals within the community; and (b) ties them as a unit, and as one, to their community *(Oha)*.

Individual life and work have meaning only within the community and the latter remains the background to individual existence and activity within any conceivable sphere. Within and among these spheres of human activity there is a regulatory principle defining the acceptable or unacceptable boundaries of good and bad: commendable or condemnable behaviour. Justice is that principle. *Omenani* is at the background of justice which is at the root of everything. It holds, binds and bonds all together.

The Igbo proverb which says that when one finger touches oil, it spreads to other fingers, soiling them indicates the idea of binding and bonding which justice performs. It means that what happens to one person affects every other person just as the entire web reverberates when one point in it is touched. The other proverb says that when the nose is affected, the eyes weep. In this sense, the idea of justice in Igbo is

---

[21] Nkeonye Otakpor, *A Sense of Justice, op. cit.,* pp. 17–18.

close to that of the early Romans where *jungere* means that "which joins or fits, a bond or tie"[22] and this easily slides into the sense of binding, fitting or bonding.

These proverbs are not about the bond of friendship but that of relationships within the community. It is like the relationship between and among the individuated points in a spider's web. The relationships are further encapsulated in a binary opposition or binary complementarity. One such relationship is that of equality and inequality.[23]

---

[22] The Romans spoke of *Jus Amicitiae* and *Jus Necessitudinis*, the bond of friendship and the bond of relationship.

[23] The diagram is from Prof. M.A. Onwuejeogwu, "An African Indigenous Ideology: Communal Individualism," An Inaugural Lecture delivered on Dec. 15, 1986, University of Benin, pp. 41 – 43. His analysis of binary relationship slightly defers from mine.

A.	The five fingers are not equal	The eagle and kite must perch together on the same tree. Anyone stopping the other would have its wings broken	AI
B.	The hand and the shoulder are on different levels	The eyes cannot see the ears though they are on the same level.	BI
C.	All trees in the forest are not equal	One tree does not make a forest. Each tree is important in making a forest what it is	CI
D.	One cannot snap the fingers without the thumb	If one finger touches oil it spreads it to the other fingers	DI

Diagram 3

In these relationships expressed proverbially and idiomatically A,B,C,D, each contradicts AI, BI, CI and DI. Furthermore, the diagram reveals that there is not only a horizontal relation of solidarity but also a vertical relation of dependence. There is a structural arrangement of contradiction and reinforcement. "It is a common feature of Igbo thought system that one kind of belief is counterbalanced by another which by opposing it moderates it in the interest of social harmony and moral good."[24]

The relationships expressed in A, B, C, D are used to show the inequality that is inevitable in any community of human beings. The causes of inequality are hinged on many factors as differentials in age, opportunity, ability, and heredity.

These proverbs expressing inequality make use of anatomical analogies. For example, the five fingers on the palm are likened to a community. The fingers are separate as individuals in a community. They are unequal in length, size and function yet they cooperate as a unit in order to achieve the objectives and goals of grasping and holding things.[25]

The five fingers are singularly and collectively responsible for the proper functioning of the hand. Thus, we can talk of the hand's (*arete*) excellence in the Aristotelian sense, if and only if, the five gingers are singularly and collectively responsible for the functioning of the hand. The thumb though regarded as the leader can only function, have meaning, in the context of, and in cooperation with, the other four.

Hence, the relationship expressed in A stresses the inequality in the community. D stresses the leadership and followership aspects of the community. D1 C1 emphasize the ideas of collective responsibility, of bonding, of binding and of ties between and among individuals. A1 stresses equality, fairness, consociation, tolerance, and accommodation.

The analogy is clear. In an Igbo community individuals live with and for one another. As Paton explains "every human being lives and acts with one another, and this offers him a unique kind of relation which can be found nowhere else."[26] In his celebrated work *African Religions and Philosophy*, Mbiti articulates this relationship much more succinctly. In his words,

> "What happens to the individual happens to the whole group, and what happens to the whole group happens to the individual. The individual can only say: I am, because we are; and since we, therefore I am."[27]

---

[24] Nkeonye Otakpor, "Social Theories and Communal Ideology," *Dialogue and Humanism*, Vol. 1, No. 1, 1994.

[25] M. A. Onwuejeogwu, *op. cit.*, p. 42.

[26] H. J. Paton, *The Good Will*, London: Allen, 1927, p. 283.

[27] J. S. Mbiti, *African Religions and Philosophy*, London: Heinemann, 1982, pp. 108 – 109.

The bonding, binding or ties implied in the idea of justice among the Igbo is at two levels (a) that between individuals, between them and the community, and (b) between value and value *(see diagram 3 at page 51)* in a general sum and a synthesis of values. Different values are necessary and focal in any organized system of human relations. There is the value of freedom, liberty, equality, cooperation, mutuality, tolerance, and dependence.

These values are an intrinsic part of the values in Igbo community like any other, and they need to be balanced against each other. They need to be ordered and reordered as circumstances demand. The claims arising from the interplay of forces need constant and insistent adjustment and readjustment. Against this background

> "it is the function of justice to adjust, join or fit these different values. Justice is the reconciler and the synthesis of these values, it is their union in an adjusted and integrated whole.[28]

Justice is the first or total value in which the others are all combined and by which they are all subjected. Justice is the ground of all other values. It is their common denominator. Justice is the only value without a denominator outside itself, because it has no reference point outside itself. It is its own reference.

---

[28] Ernest Baker, *Principles of Social and Political Theory*, Oxford: University Press, 1967, p. 102.

Chapter 4

The meaning of justice

The norm of justice

In all societies justice is a norm with the sole aim of securing the minimal ordering of relations. To achieve this goal, the Igbo long before colonial rule and the establishment of the Nigerian state, created their own internal legality. The Igbo judicial system predates both because Igbo culture is older than the colonial culture as well as the emergent Nigerian culture, if there is any. Igbo justice and legality is parallel to (and sometimes conflicting with) the legality of the defunct colonial administration. Three decades after Nigeria's independence, the same relationship holds between Igbo justice and legality *vis-a-vis* the one that obtains in the Nigerian state of which the Igbo is part thereof.

Theirs has been a kind of popular justice imbued with a wide distribution of legal skills as expressed in the absence of professionalism, easy accessibility and participation, non-coercive justice as expressed in the absence of professionalism and the orientation towards consensus.

Justice among the Igbo is far more than an ordinary concept. It is far more than a yardstick for the measurement of individual conduct or for the determination of desert. For them, justice is at the root of life. It is the foundation of all there is.

Igbo society is not different in this respect, yet the meaning of justice for them is not exactly the same as in other cultures. There are peculiarities and differences dictated by the nuances in Igbo community.

While the analysis of lexical and syntactic meaning within Igbo language expressions may be fruitful and is necessary for a thorough understanding and appreciation of the concept's multi-layered meanings, it is the discourse and pragmatic dimensions of its use which bring substantial accretions to its meaning. Thus to understand the concept of justice and the way meaning inheres in it, it will be much more rewarding to analyse its usage in Igbo language and culture.

In the preceding chapter it was established that there is no single Igbo word which completely explains the concept of justice. It was found that the root idea of justice can only be gleaned from a conjunction of words, or in an assemblage of words or phrases. By the same token the meaning of justice in Igbo cannot be found in a single word but in a conjunction of words or in an assemblage of words or phrases.

Three Igbo words put together give ample indication of this; *ugwo, ne* and *olu.* From these three words the following are derivable.

a) *Ugwo olu;*
b) *Ne olu*
c) *Mkpulu onye kuu*

All three have the same reference in terms of desert or lot.

Your desert: *Ugwo olu*

Ugwo olu means "wages, salary, payment for work done."[1] The relevant issue is neither salary, wages nor payment but reward for work done or undone, in terms of act or omission. Hence the statement: *onye obuna ga ana ugwo olu,* meaning that everybody will receive a reward for work done or undone. Put differently, it means that there is desert for act or omission.

Nee olu

There is also reward as in *ne olu,* that is, reward for work done or not done or work not satisfactorily done.

---

[1] Kay Williamson, *op. cit.,* p. 418.

The person who does good works: *onye olu oma,* earns not only praises but material rewards as the case may be, whether here or hereafter. The concern is double-edged. Anyone regarded as *onye olu oma* is equally a good person. The goodness has a multiplier effect and transcends the present life. Hence the concern is not solely with the desert available in this world but with the ultimate one, hereafter.

The insistence and encouragement on doing the good and the right, is in the final analysis, not directed at the good life here only but the hereafter as well.

The value of a good name and the maintenance of a worthy pedigree, *Mkpulu madu,* is important as well as necessary because a good name is better than all the material wealth in this world. The Igbo believe that human beings only share a good name with birds and animals like *Awolo/Agu* (Lion), *Egbe* (Eagle). No human being in his or her proper senses will take the name of *Ewu* (goat) or *Okwukwu/Okuko* (fowl).

Because of issues closely associated with reincar-nation, the Igbo are also deeply concerned with divine and human justice. While this is undoubtedly true, it is nonetheless obvious that their concern is tilted more in the direction of divine justice because of the imperfections in human nature, and because of their insistence that pure, absolute justice is possible in the divine realm. For them only *Chi ukwu* (God) can dispense justice in an absolute and pure manner.

According to Okafor, divine justice has the following features: (a) "It is impartial, (b) it is absolute, (c) it is immutable, (d) it is not bound by space and time."[2] For the Igbo, the highest court of justice is *Chi ukwu* (God) who is spoken of in highly superlative terms. Human justice can never be final or absolute, can never be the best because of the precariousness of the human condition, and because of the finiteness of history at the individual and collective levels of our being.

What kind of *olu* (work) is under reference? It is work manifested in act or omission in relations between persons and between persons, and the community. It is work in terms of:

a) being a good neighbour and being your brother's keeper;
b) doing community work of various kinds, that is, doing civic duties;
c) giving assistance to the needy, the aged and to all those unable to fend for themselves because of one reason or the other;
d) adherence to community standards of behaviour in moral, religious

---

[2] F.U. Okafor, *op. cit.,* p. 40.

and political matters, that is, behaviour that is in accord with the dictates, precepts and standards as per the demands of *Omenani;*
e) observance of the community standards of objectivity;
f) telling the truth always no matter the issue and the circumstances.

Persons who live in strict compliance with the above are judged as living in compliance with the dictates of *Omenani,* and are judged to be the embodiment of goodness, kindness, sincerity, truth and morality. They are the persons who have *ezi omume,* that is, who are righteous and of good deeds. They are exemplars of goodness, righteousness and truth, that is, *Ezigbo madu.* They are the persons who know the truth and uphold it no matter what, that is, *ndi ezi okwu,* plural; *onye ezi okwu,* singular.

For obvious reasons, truth, righteousness, sincerity, etc., in relation to act or omission are structurally linked to justice. An evil, unrighteous and insincere person may not be truthful and may not be just. The desire for truth and justice arising from the inner compulsion to follow the dictates of *Omenani* is most often not manifested in those who are evil, unrighteous and insincere.

The deviant persons in Igbo community are those who do evil things, who do "bad work" in their relationships with others, that is, *ndi ajo olu.* They obey and adhere strictly, either by design or accident, to the norms totally and completely opposed to those of the community. They are identified as people who are:

a) unkind – *afo njo;*
b) bad, wicked, evil, niggardly – *ndi njo* or *ndi afo njo;*
c) most often, they are driven by selfish and myopic impulses.

Persons who live this kind of life out of their own choice or through circumstances beyond their control are for the Igbo, unrighteous, unkind, untruthful, evil minded, and cannot be entrusted with leadership roles in the community. They may not be just in their dealings with other people. Again, for the Igbo, unkindness, insincerity, unrighteousness and falsehood are structurally linked to injustice. An unkind, unrighteous, untruthful and insincere person cannot be impartial, cannot be objective in terms of community standards, and cannot be just.

What is the reward for unkindness, unrighteousness, untruthfulness and lack of sincerity? The reward is here and hereafter. The evil that men do does not live after them only. The evil that men do lives with them and before them. Hence, those who escape from their just rewards here have no escape hereafter. They have no escape from God's final reward because God is the final arbiter in the affairs of human beings. *Chi nwe okwu.* God has the last, the final word in the affairs of human beings.

Unjust persons do not live a good life and are unworthy of respect. Such persons may be materially well off yet by their fruits they are known. Though materially comfortable they have no peace because peace is incompatible with evil. They have difficulty in getting a wife or husband as decent members of the community subtly dissociate themselves from such persons. By their own wilful choice unjust persons place an embargo on their right to live in harmony with the living and dead members of the community. They place an embargo on their inherent right to reincarnate which in itself "is a good thing, it is a return to this sunlit world for further period of invigorating life."[3] They lose their right to be among the ancestors. They are outcasts here and hereafter. Such a person is "the man to whom other human beings are not good, this implies that such an individual must either correct himself or be unacceptable to the community."[4]

Yet unrighteous, evil, insincere and unjust persons are not entirely lost to an Igbo community. The community never completely abandons the unrighteous, unjust and evildoer. Such acts or omission are neither condoned nor are the miscreants hidden away or allowed to escape. Instead the community exerts its paternalistic authority in the sense of preventing the individual from further harm to self and to the community. One widely current Igbo proverb says it all, "a kinsman who strays into evil must first be saved from it by all, then afterwards be questioned on why and how he dared stray into it, to start with."[5]

On the individual, family or interpersonal levels there are redemptive steps intended to bring back a kinsman who has strayed. Conscious of public opinion, *onu oha* or *onu madu*, that is what others will say, attempts are made towards redirection of a strayed kinsman. There are common proverbs that express the feeling of uneasiness in this regard:

a) Shame is for the mad man's relation, not for the mad man himself;
b) A man whose relation dances out of rhythm and very badly normally

---

[3] E.G. Parrinder, *Afrinca Traditional Religion,* London: S.P.C.K., 1962.

[4] E. M. P. Edeh, *op. cit.* p. 106.

[5] Ibid., p.106.

had twitches of the eye-lids;
c) A friend or a relation of a thief or bad person always feels very
   ashamed.

Injustice fractures the rhythm of community life. It truncates the
wholeness of community life. Since Igbo community is founded on
brotherhood and the oneness of community life, it is easy to discern the
community concern over evil and injustice, even when these are
individualized. It is also easy to discern the concern of friends and
immediate relations since individual life has meaning only in relation to
what the community is or is not, in terms of its ill or good fortunes.
Evil, wrongdoing, falsehood, etc., are isolationistic, individually and
collectively. They impact decidedly on individuals who are close to the
offender. To minimize this impact or even avoid it altogether if
possible, the Igbo believe that the community "will not condone evil or
maltreatment of others by another. It must speak out against evil talk or
deed."[6]

Mkpulu onye kuu ka oga agho: We reap what we sow.

This Karmic principle or law is expressed under different guises in the
various religions and philosophies of the world. But it is certainly no
stranger to any of them, by whatever name it may be called.
     None of the traditions in the world denies it; each in one way or
another explicitly affirms it. It has a place in every culture.
     In the spiritual realm as in the physical, this principle applies. For
the Igbo it applies in this world and the next. In other words,
reincarnation only makes sense in conjunction with the principle. The
other reason is that Igbo metaphysics is overly deterministic; every
event has a cause and every cause has its effects. For the Igbo human life
is cyclic.
     Mkpulu onye kuu is logically and metaphysically equivalent to *Ife
Onye nye ani, Ka ani nenye ya* in terms of meaning. The principle
means that there is reward for every act or omission either in this world

---

[6] P.K. Davids *The Text Book of Igbo Proverbs*, Onitsha: University Publishing 1980, p.
   136.

or the next. If your reward, due or lot is not available in this world, it is available in the next circle of life.

Hence, we reap what we sow expresses the fundamental moral principle in a basic form. It also expresses a fundamental legal principle in a basic form.

To live by the sword is to perish by the sword. This is not entirely retributive because it has echoes of the basic principle. By an inexorable moral law, every act or omission has consequences: good acts have good consequences, bad acts bad consequences. Edwin Arnold poetically expressed this as follows:

> ...my brother's! each mans life,
> The outlook of his former living is;
> The bygone wrongs bring forth sorrows and woes,
> The bygone right breeds bliss.[7]

These consequences may be immediate, in the short or in the long term. There is no escape from the good or bad consequences of act or omission. This applies with equal force to communities collectively regarded in this case as moral agents or legal persons.

For the Igbo when bad consequences are perceived, oracles are consulted and the gods are propitiated in order to (a) avert it, or (b) minimize the effects. But this is equivalent to a postponement of an evil day that must come. Given the nature and operations of this principle, it is clear that such propitiations do not work. They do not accomplish the objectives of those who engage in them.

For the perception of good consequences, the gods are also propitiated in order to (a) ensure that it does happen, (b) that it happens in good times, and (c) that it brings other benefits.

The principle is at the core of all deeply religious and philosophic thought. It affects life at every point and every turn. It is at the core of justice since justice is the root of life. It is the principle of duty, the balance that lies at the core of all things and is so fundamental, so inexorable, that not even the most basic physical laws we know of can be so immutable.

---

[7] Sir Edwin Arnold, *Light of Asia,* Book 8.

Truth is Life

Truth, sincerity and righteousness are isormorphically related to justice. This is expressed lucidly in the following two statements:

a) *Eziokwu bu ndu:* Truth is life [True word is life].
b) It is better to be a spendthrift than to be a rogue.

Ezi as a neutral noun means goodness, right, truth. Hence:

a) *Ezi madu:* good person
b) *Ezi omume:* good deeds, righteousness
c) *Ezi okwu:* true word (statement)
d) *Ezie:* truly; is it right?
e) *Kwu eziokwu:* tell the truth. Make a statement that is true.

Truth is life is not in reference to material and mundane enjoyment of life. The basic reference is to truth and it is in terms of its essence to human life. Truth is not just life; it is the essence of life. Human beings are remembered not because of their material possessions or because of other worldly possessions or the lack thereof. They are often remembered for the kind of life they lived in terms of their passion for telling the truth, their total commitment to the community standards of objectivity and impartiality in their dealings with others.

The notion that truth is life is concomitant with the idea that justice is at the root of life. Justice is at the root of life because truth is the essence of life. Truth is the ground of our being for without it all else is lost in chaos, anarchy and war with the attendant social and cultural disequilibrium. A community where truth and justice are not basic to the lives of its members is headed for cultural suicide and possible disintegration.

There is an Igbo expression concerning this. It is that "when one cheek chews and the other did not chew, that other cheek is not happy.[8] This means that partiality spoils management and administration. By extension it is not only partiality that can bring about this situation. Insincerity, unrighteousness, dishonesty, can lead to bad management and administration of community affairs. It is obvious that an impartial person is at the same time dishonest, insincere and unrighteous. Such a

---

[8] Ibid., p. 149.

person can not be objective and cannot be expected to be truthful and just. He cannot be entrusted with the management of community affairs.

Oath taking

Oath means *Ikwu iyi/Igba iyi/Inu iyi*, and is administered to ensure that members of the community live according to the norms, rules, regulations, and conventional practices enshrined in *Omenani*. It is a means of regulating conduct. It is a means of ensuring that truth and justice prevail. It helps to establish truth, guilt or innocence. According to Nwala it "is a form of ritual treaty designed to ensure transparency in dealing with one's neighbour, of discouraging lying and other evils in the community."[9]

This is most profound because a life that is not lived in accordance with the demands and requirements of *Omenani* of the Igbo is a wasted one. Such a person is regarded as *anu manu* or *anu ofia*, a derisive remark, which has echoes of the Socratean pig.

Oath is administered as a reminder of the oneness of life in the community and to revivify the common faith in a destiny that is commonly sourced and shared. A person who refuses to take oath or who has problems as a result of the oath taking is an evil, dishonest, unrighteous and unjust person. Such a person lives outside the dictates of *Omenani*, is not a good person and does not live a good life.

A good life, that is, a life lived in compliance with *Omenani* is all that is needed to be a good person, a good neighbour, a brother's keeper. It is all that is needed for the acute development and nourishment of a sense of community, which enables someone to be accepted by the ancestors at death, and to be remembered at crucial moments by kinsmen who are still trading in the world, because *Uwa bu afia*, that is, the world is a market-place.[10]

Oath taking is not only a universal phenomenon and practice, it is an inherent part of any human culture. It is an essential component of any justice system.

---

[9] T.U. Nwala, *op. cit.*, p. 73. The administration of oath as a method of judicial ascertainment of truth is not peculiar to Igbo people. Oath taking is universal.

[10] Nkeonye Otakpor, "The World is a Market-Place," *Journal of Value Inquiry*, Vol. 30, No. 4, 1996, pp. 521-530.

For example, in *Onyenge* v. *Ebere (2004), All Federation Weekly Law Report* at 981–1001, the Supreme Court held that Oath taking is a valid process under customary law arbitration. It is one of the methods of establishing the truth of a matter and was known to customary law.

The Court further argued that where two parties to a dispute voluntarily submit the issue in a controversy between them to an arbitration (through oath taking) according to customary law and agree expressly or by implication that the decision of such arbitration would be accepted as final and binding, then once the arbitrators reach a decision, it would no longer be open to either party to subsequently back out from the decision so pronounced.

Chapter 5

The principles of Igbo law

What are these principles?

The principles of law in Aniocha Igbo culture are many. However, only a few are selected here for analysis. The selection is not arbitrary because these principles are foci in the determination of a just desert. These principles are also important because their absence, misapplication, misconception or ill-use can inevitably lead to unjust decisions with the consequent chaos and social disequilibrium.

It is interesting to note the fact that these principles are also part of the colonial and post-colonial legal system of Nigeria. They are found in other legal systems, either in whole or in part.

It must be emphasised that these principles, as known to the Igbo, are not adaptations or variants of the colonial or post colonial ones in Nigeria or elsewhere. The principles are indigenous to Igbo culture and tradition. They are part and parcel of Igbo culture, tradition and worldview, beginning from the pagan inception of human history, recorded and unrecorded.

Igbo norms, principles and rules are unwritten but they are fossilized in their legal idioms and proverbs which are orally transmitted from generation to generation. So are legal concepts undefined in precise terms as in modern nation-states. The most viable way is that of finding points of view whose general acceptance is capable of rendering a piece of reasoning convincing and the conclusion acceptable.

Such points of view in Igbo are many but the most important ones are:

1. *Madu aya aha eghe enye onwe-e.* No person should be a judge in his or her own cause;
2. *Onye mefie ka ikpe ma.* There is no wrong without remedy. Guilt, not accident, is what makes people liable;
3. *Njo egbu mkpulu obi, obuna so ajo omume.* An act does not itself constitute guilt unless the mind is guilty;
4. *Onye da iwu me njo.* There is no crime except in accordance with the law;
5. *Onye me njo agba oso ma wa achuna.* No freeman shall be arrested or detained without a trial;
6. *Waya anu onu ofuonye we aha eghe.* The imperative of fair hearing or due process. Always listen to both sides before any decision;
7. *Madu ama li ulu dina njo ome.* No man may profit from his own wrongdoing or take advantage of his own wrongdoing, or make any claims upon his own iniquity, or acquire property from his own crime;
8. *Me – em kawa me ibem.* This is the principle of equality. Literally this means: treat me like others in the same class or group to which I belong. Not to be treated like others leads to confusion and arbitrariness. It is the principle of equality before the law;
9. *Ife onye kpe kawa aha nye.* Facts and issues not pleaded or presented in evidence should neither be allowed nor accepted in a settlement;
10. *Wa kpochi uzo ha eghe, we Kpopu uzo, eghe apuha ilo.* The terms of settlement must be supported by good reasons especially those reasons that meet the community's standard of fairness, impartiality, objectivity and truth;
11. *Oha ka madu.* Public good is always to be preferred to private or individual interests;
12. *Wa ya ezu oshi ewe eme ogo* or *Ife onye nwe ka oji eme ogo.* Nobody can give to others what he or she does not have. Nobody can transfer to others more rights than he has;
13. *Wa ya ewe iwe egbu oni.* Anger is not guilt;
14. *Emena madu ife wa ama me-e.* The Golden Rule. Do unto others…Treat others with the same consideration as you would have them treat you;
15. *Egbe belu, ugo belu.* Live and let live principle. It means the kite should perch, the eagle should also perch.

These points of view are properly regarded as principles. Though unwritten they are not alien to the Igbo mind. They are not products of colonialism because they are enshrined in *Omenani.*

These principles are based on reason and are intended to convince. They refer to what is evident and to public policy. They are based on community knowledge, experience and wisdom, and the system of logic inherent in Igbo tradition. They are based on common sense, on the common good, and on the demands and imperatives of the public interest. In a broader sense, they refer to areas of social agreement and the norms which they embrace appear to be self-evident.

They function as aggregating standards of measure for conduct and help to induce agreement and consensus in those areas where uncertainty may be prevalent. As insights or guideposts that orient the resolution of conflicts, they point to elements that are not controversial.

Since they are general, they appear vague and tend to invest speech with duplicity of meaning. To regard them in this light may lead to distortion because their content emerges graphically in their application to specific legal problems. How these principles function in the resolution of conflicts is the main issue dealt with in the next chapter.

What follows is an attempt to explain the meaning of some of these principles and their relevance to Igbo traditional justice system. The other principles not dealt with are no less important in terms of the argumentative and rhetorical needs of the justice system.

Equality before the law

Me-em kawa me ibem (treat me exactly like others in the same class, or category or group to which I belong). This is the principle of equality and inequality. It means that individuals who are equals must not be treated as unequals and those who are unequals must not be treated as equals.

This explanation is neither sufficient nor exhaustive. The principle extends beyond the treatment of persons as equals or as unequals. It means equality before the law. It ensures that persons in the same class, group, or category are treated alike. It ensures that there is no discrimination based on arbitrary indices or grounds that run counter to the demands and imperatives of *Omenani.*

In the determination of desert, the use of the principle ensures that there is equality of reward for the work done or not done. It means that like cases or situations are treated alike or that similar cases or situations are treated similarly.

The idea that equals should not be treated as unequals and *vice versa* does not mean that there is no ranking or hierarchical order in an

Igbo community. Igbo society is not a classless society in Marxian terms. There is hierarchical order which is based on biological age, achievement resulting from individual effort, distinctive character traits, and professional competence such as in war, medicine or the performance of the appropriate ceremonies for *Okpala* title or some other chieftaincy title recognised and reckoned with in the various Igbo communities. Igbo communities value these and more and individuals are respected primarily because they are human beings and as such deserve respect and secondarily because of their position in the society.

The performance of the prescribed rites and ceremonies leading to the conferment of the *okpala* chieftaincy title, for example, puts one in the class of *okpala* titled men. Within that class, there is a hierarchical order in terms of when one performed the prescribed ceremonies. *Okpala* titled men are a class of their own and members expect to be treated on equal terms. Where the need arises for differential treatment, there is a procedure to be followed and reasons are given. The tradition of *Okpala* titled men, in such matters, is religiously observed in order to avoid injustice and the confusion that follows it.

In the wider Igbo society, *okpala* titled men have their place and function, and are accorded the respect due to them as individuals and as a class. What applies to members of *okpala* titled men as a class applies to other groups in an Igbo community, and what applies to individual members of *okpala* association applies to other members of Igbo community as individuals. In an Igbo community, therefore, it is simply a matter of to each person, his or her due. Socio-economic and cultural standing in the community is of value and is respected but is not more important in terms of the treatment and respect of individuals on the basis of our common humanity. Each of us has his or her origin in the common source of life.

There are problems in the actual application of this principle. The first problem and the most relevant and profound is that it contradicts the wisdom embodied in the saying that the five fingers on the palm are not equal. This emphasises the inequality in nature and in the community. In chapter one, the import of the inequality epitomised by the five fingers in terms of size, function, individually and collectively was highlighted. This was linked to a community comprising individuals who are unequal in natural endowments, talents, physical strength, moral disposition, etc.

The contradiction is one of terms, not material. The fact that the five fingers are not equal is a recognition and a tacit acknowledgement of inequality which is inevitable in the conduct of human affairs. To insist on treating equals as equals, not as unequals; and unequals as unequals, not as equals is to ameliorate the socio-economic and cultural impact of inequality. It is intended as a poignant reminder of the fact that though inequality is natural, unavoidable and perhaps indispensable, the community need not be held hostage to the consequences attendant on its cold and chilly application.

To treat equals on equal terms and unequals on unequal terms ensures that no person is marginalised on account of age, distinction, history, achievement or professional efficiency. It is a subtle way of according recognition and respect for the station of each person, no matter what that station is, in real and material terms. In the determination of desert, it ensures that persons get their lot or due irrespective of age, station, history, achievement and professional standing.

Furthermore, the maxim of the five fingers is analogously related to the station and function of individuals in an Igbo community, specifically related to individuals *qua* individuals. Instead of taking them as contradictory pairs, they are, perhaps, better regarded as complementary. Equality and inequality complement each other since each operates from one side of the same coin.

To insist on treating individuals in the same class in the same way is germane to the mechanism employed in dispute settlement. Similar cases are treated similarly and individual desert, though difficult to measure appropriately, is supposed to be the same. Without this, injustice prevails.

It becomes the rule rather than the exception. To avoid this development, precedents are cited as a reminder of how a present dispute is similar to a previous one.

Once this similarity is established, the same principle or principles are evoked. The decision in the present case would then be similar and the desert is at the same time similar, if the *anteceding* causal facts are also similar. In such situations the usual questions are: What did we do before? *Gini ka anyi me mbu?* How did we do it then? *Kaka anyi si me-e?* What decision or decisions were taken?

These questions and their answers, and the mechanisms for dispute settlement, using this principle, are encapsulated in the Igbo proverb which says that a human corpse is neither novel nor alien to earth: *Ozu abuna ani ife ofu.* The answers to these questions ensure that arbitrariness is minimised, when not avoided completely.

In novel situations, often aptly expressed in the statement: *anyi afunene nkeni (onwo) mbu,* that is, we have not seen or heard this kind of thing before, the stock of community knowledge and wisdom is at the disposal of those involved in decision making. *Omenani* may not provide a comprehensive guide to thought and action in such novel situations, but its reliance and use is clearly unavoidable. The general principles enshrined in *Omenani* are evoked, reformulated and reshaped to suit the problem at hand. As Nwala puts it, in such "moments new ideas can emerge and a precedence is set, or old ideas could be expounded or reformulated."[1]

To treat equals on the same terms and unequals on the same terms, also implies even-handedness and impartiality. Impartiality: *enene madu anya nihu,* is a precondition for objectivity in the conduct of human affairs.

Impartiality means detachment from personal likes and dislikes, from vested interests, primordial loyalties and orientations in order to establish in a given situation what the case is: *Nofu ka odi.* It implies the lack of consideration of what a person is or is not.

Without impartiality the road to truth is clogged, blurred and perhaps remains unexplored and unknown. Without the knowledge of truth, justice cannot be done. The determination of individual reward, *okem,* is impossible to achieve unless the truth concerning the situation in known. Truth is, therefore, a precondition for justice.

Impartiality does not mean that there are no personal interests worthy of pursuit, or that we cannot be passionate, jealous, loving and hateful any more. This is far from what is demanded by the insistence that equals and unequals be treated in the same manner if justice is to be done to the members of the same class. Impartiality means applying the same norms, rules and principles *(Omenani)* consistently irrespective of personal interest and emotional attachment or involvement.

Impartiality is central to moral life: *ezi ndu,* in all its aspects. It has an overriding regulative role in all aspects of morality. It is a successful resistance to the vice of bias and prejudice in making and acting upon critical judgements.

Impartiality is necessary but not sufficient for strictly objective judgement because obstacles other than bias and prejudice may still prevent one from judging correctly. The natural limits of intelligence or imagination may impair judgement of even scrupulously impartial agents and so, when lapses are to be explained in that way, accusation of bias and prejudice are misplaced.

It also amounts to a blind egalitarianism, guaranteed to avoid havoc in a situation where alertness to morally relevant differences between persons is needed. Here, the connection between impartiality and

---

[1] T.U. Nwala, *op. cit.,* p. 10.

equality is closer than the relation of impartiality to other standards or principles found in *Omenani.*

The conflation of impartiality with the principle of equality is easy to understand. Given the widely held belief among the Igbo that human beings are equal, have equal moral worth, we naturally suppose that in the more difficult task of practical deliberation, such as the design of the conception of justice, some principle of equality will constitute the right standard of impartial judgement. There is reason to expect damaging consequences where this is not the case.

Impartiality is also linked to integrity or authenticity for a people to whom community life really matters. A partial judgement or standpoint is thus a signal of lack of integrity. A misplaced concern with impartiality has a withering effect upon the Igbo sense of life's goal and meaning. It is not an indispensable ally to its role in the Igbo conception of the good life.

Impartiality makes the vast differences between human beings legally and morally irrelevant. A case for partial treatment can be allowed but a case has to be made for it: the experiences of illness and old age and the situations of the very young, the widow and the orphan are good grounds for such a case.

When equals are not treated on the same terms or when unequals are treated equally or when individuals in the same category or class are arbitrarily selected for the differential treatment, the result is social conflict and disharmony. The social conflict may be traced to either one or all of the following:

1. the partial and incomplete application of rules, standards and norms pertaining to a class, category or social position as embodied in *Omenani;*
2. the attempt to alter the width of the social cluster to which certain rules and norms apply in order to accommodate the partiality and inconsistency;
3. the imbalance resulting from the division of the class or category into we *(anyi)* and them *(wa).*

Even-handedness is at the core of justice among the Igbo. It implies that norms, rules and principles are applied to every member of the social group consistently and indifferently, in action and in judgement. Differential treatment is justified only by reference to relevant differences of attribute or condition, that is, differences recognised by the rules and principles embodied in *Omenani.*

Onye obuna gana ugwo olu-a

Which means "to each according to his or her moral goodness" is justice and nothing short of this can be regarded as just. To each, his/her own moral goodness is a principle unrestricted in its application to many different situations. There are limitations, however, because there is nothing like equalization of talent, merit, obligation, rights and duties. Yet, reward is given on the basis of merit, demerit, excellence or need. Even this cannot be achieved without strictly complying with the principle: to each his/her own.

Live and let live

Egbe belu, Ugo belu: (the kite and the eagle each has a right to perch on the same tree. Anyone denying the other this right must have its wings broken, that is, loses the right to perch).

This expresses the desire for equity, fairness, consociation, accommodation and tolerance. It is, in very simple and popular sense all that is implied in the live and let live principle.

Two critical issues are raised by the application of this maxim in relation to justice. These are (a) equal rights and (b) non-interference.

The maxim has direct reference to a community of people with the usual diversity of interests and desires each in opposition to the other. The maxim seeks to demonstrate that while an Igbo community welcomes and indeed encourages healthy competition because the competitive capitalist spirit has never been ossified in the Igbo communal way of life, there is room for tolerance, accommodation, mutuality and peaceful co-existence.

Justice is necessary for order and peaceful co-existence because *Udoka ogwu mma:* which means that peace is preferable to disorder, anarchy and war. To ensure and guarantee peace there must be justice, and to ensure and guarantee justice there must be respect for individual rights, personal tastes, and interests of individuals.

There must be respect for the law of the land: *Iwu obodo* as enunciated in *Omenani.* Any person who wilfully interferes with the rights, privileges, and interests of others loses his or her own rights, interests and privileges.

Respect for the rights, privileges, and interests of others; and non-interference with other people's rights, freedom, and liberty make for healthy and peaceful co-existence. In the words of Okafor:

> "in the terse but lucid proverbial statement of value, the social doctrine of the Igbo is encapsuled. In essence, the doctrine sets out to state the principles which if adhered to will promote social justice and foster social harmony, and political stability. For peaceful co-existence among men to be possible, men must learn not to interfere with people's rights and liberty."[2]

Okafor's perspective lucidly exemplifies the basic idea in "live and let live", for without adherence to this basic idea all else is conflict. On a superficial reading this principle appears to be very individualistic. It appears to run counter to the communal spirit that typifies Igbo life style and worldview.

This is only an appearance and remains so. At the deeper layers of the social, political, cultural, religious, and economic life, the basic structures that support life and activities in Igbo community are communal in nature. Mbiti perhaps had the Igbo in mind when he argued that:

> "what happens to the individual happens to the whole group and whatever happens to the whole group happens to the individual."[3]

In the traditional Igbo worldview, the individual is neither socially nor culturally atomised. He exists as a member of the community, that is, he exists corporately, communally and commensally. The insistence on non-interference and on respect for the rights, liberty and freedom of every person is, therefore, not a subtle way of promoting individualism. *Oha ka madu,* that is, the community is greater, better, and fuller, does not mean that the community is tyrannically inclined. The emphasis on the community is not a diminution of the importance of individuals qua individuals. Otakpor has suggested that "non-individualism as a social value is not the same as anti-individualism. An

---

[2] F. U. Okafor, *op. cit.,* p. 89.

[3] J. S. Mbiti, *op. cit.,* pp. 108-109.

Igbo community is not anti-individualist though it is to a large extent, based on non-individualism."[4]

The individual is reckoned with in terms of his or her contributions to the commonwealth. To achieve this goal, liberty, freedom and rights are priced and respected. Beyond this the individual is a social being and is part of the whole. Mbiti again suggests that,

> "just as God made the first man, as God's man, so now man himself make the individual who becomes the corporate or social man. Only in terms of other people does the individual become conscious of his own being, his own duties, his privileges and responsibilities towards himself and towards other people."[5]

Egbe belu, Ugo belu, is a social mechanism for safeguarding the right, privileges, liberty and freedom of individuals. Without this safeguard the inherent natural inclination of a human being towards self-centredness, egoism and unbridled individualism with their socially destructive tendencies would be allowed free and unfettered reign. This is inimical to collective interest.

Igbo kwenu which symbolises that collective, communal, or corporate will of the Igbo will be subsumed under *mmu kwenu* which symbolises unbridled individualism. The worth of individual personhood is, nonetheless, important in terms of self-dependent value judgements. Our willingness to make and carry through self-dependent value judgements is plainly vital to the survival of Igbo families, friendship, and communities united by a sense of common destiny and loyalty.

Fair hearing

Waya anu onu ofuonye aha eghe. This is the principle of fair hearing and due process. The practical application of this principle is explained in detail in the subsection on dispute settlement in the next chapter.

---

[4] Andrew Isiguzo and Nkeonye Otakpor, "Communalism and Paternalism in Igbo Culture," *International Journal of African Culture and Ideas,* Vol. 2, Nos. 1 and 2, 1999.

[5] J. S. Mbiti, *op. cit.,* p. 108.

The principle makes it mandatory and obligatory, that the two sides of a story or dispute are heard before a decision is taken. It means that both sides to a dispute are heard together and in an open court. It emphasises that no morally and legally just decision can be taken when only one side to a dispute has been heard.

Elders (at any level of decision making) and the council exercise judicial functions which require them to give parties a fair hearing and to reach decisions on the merits of their cases based on the facts adduced.

Fundamentally, it means that those in dispute must be given equal opportunity to state their cases and defend themselves before decisions are arrived at, and judgement given. It is a principle of natural justice among the Igbo that just as a story is dualistic in nature so is a dispute. A dispute is a kind of story and like a coin, it is dualistic in nature. To that extent, a one-sided estimate is avoided by ensuring that both sides are heard simultaneously.

No matter how serious an offence is, and no matter how heinous a crime is, the suspect, as a prerequisite to the proper and adequate determination of guilt or innocence, must first be heard. To insist on reaching a decision and on determining desert without fair hearing amounts to partiality. It amounts to reaching an unfair decision, which is unjust.

Disputants are therefore required to state their own side of a story, to question the persons on the other side, to cross examine witnesses, and to reject persons who they think incompetent to serve as jurors during the process of decision making.

To refuse to hear from all sides, or to insist on hearing only from one side instead of both, amounts to a betrayal of standards. To betray standards out of malice *(ajo onunu)*, anger *(iwe)* or misplaced compassion represents bias and prejudice.

Yet we cannot expunge out desires, passions and sentiments, only that we refuse to reckon with them, or let them dictate the content of our judgements. The suppression of bias and prejudice does not require the suppression of the emotion and desire that lie behind them. In this and other spheres of Igbo life, the exercise of virtue *(ezigbo amala)* requires impartiality.

The Golden Rule

The golden rule enjoins that you treat others, as you would like them to treat you. 'Do unto others as you would have them do unto you' *(Matt. 7:12)*. Emphasis is essentially on impartiality, reminding each person not to treat himself as a special case. Fair consideration and treatment should be extended to all irrespective of political association, religion and social status. As Hospers puts it, "don't treat yourself as a special case, be as impartial in considering what you should do as you would be in deciding what someone quite unknown to you should do."[6]

Matthew 7:12, popularised the rule among Christian denominations. Not only has the rule been popularised, it also acquired an overly religious baggage in terms of meaning.

While this religious connotation has to be reckoned with, the fact that the golden rule predates any organised religion is trite. It is part of the cultural heritage of humanity down the ages. It was not invented or coined to primarily serve any particular religious purpose or purposes. The fact that the rule is popular in religious circles does not impeach its secular origins. Its development is consequent on the vagaries of life and on human experience of the same.

As an important rule of conduct, the golden rule is avowedly part of the moral code that human beings observe wherever they are.

Among the Igbo, the rule translates thus: *emena madu ife wa ama me nginwa*. This means that, in principle as well as in practice, no one should subject another person to any kind of treatment for which one would normally feel angry, resentment, or unhappiness. For example, if one would feel bad on being cheated, then one should avoid cheating others. One should not contemplate cheating on others; to do this, means to enthrone a double standard.

It follows, therefore, that any breach of the golden rule amounts to a double standard. Double standards are to be avoided like a plague. Justice cannot be done where double talk and double think constitute the standards. The use of a double standard will necessarily lead to inconsistency, to lack of regard for the feelings of others, and to partiality. Wherever these are in place the result is injustice, not justice.

The Igbo believe that what one would not desire, wish or want for himself/herself, should not be wished, desired, or wanted for other human beings. The prayers one is not willing to say to the ancestors and God for one's progress, good, and general well-being are on the same grounds not to be said for any other person, known or unknown. These are social and cultural articles of faith in a system that believes that the human race is one: *anyi bu ofu*.

---

[6] John Hospers, *An Introduction to Philosophical Analysis*, London: Routledge and Kegan Paul, 1970, p. 597.

For the Igbo, there is no life for those who are ever thinking of *themselves* and forgetting all other *selves*. Life groans under the weight of such selfish consideration and concentration. Lack of consideration of the feelings, desires, wants, and the overall well-being of others is morally unacceptable. And justice cannot thrive in a situation that is predicated on the absence of such considerations.

The Golden Rule is not exclusive to Christianity and Igbo traditions. It is inherent in other traditions. There is no human group that has no idea of the Golden Rule or a human group where this principle does not occupy an important place in the conduct of affairs, public and private.

The following are examples of the most famous ones among them:

- What is hateful to you, do not do to your neighbour, (Judaism);
- What you do not want done to yourself, do not do unto others, (Confucianism);
- Let no man do to another that which would be repugnant to himself, (Hinduism);
- Hurt not others in ways that you yourself would find hurtful, (Buddhism);
- Do to others as you would have them do unto you, (Christianity, *Matt. 7:12*);
- *Emena madu ife wa ama me nginwa,* (Igbo).

It is no surprise that the Golden Rule is, indeed, a truly universal principle.

Presumption

This literally translates as *olika ya mee-e:* "It seems ..." For the Igbo, justice cannot be based on "it seems", that is, on the presumption of guilt. Presumption means something which seems likely although there is no proof. For the Igbo, guilt must be proven, not presumed or assumed. No one can be found guilty without the proof of evidence.

No man is allowed to be a judge in his own cause

No man should be a judge in his own cause in Igbo, translates thus: *madu aya eghe enye onwe-e.* The reason is that his interest will certainly bias his judgement, and probably, corrupt his integrity. No one can be judge and jury at the same time.

Second, there is likely to be neither impartiality nor objectivity, the kind that is required in order for justice is done. Third, truth may be the most important casualty whereas one essential requirement for justice, among the Igbo, is that the truth must be told, and this always. Truth is of the essence of a good life, in the administration of communal affairs, and therefore in the determination of guilt or innocence in any given situation. Justice in the absence of truth; it is a recipe for chaos.

Fourth, an Igbo proverb instructs that no one cleans his own wound or sore and weeps at the same time. In other words, a man who is his own judge is unlikely to be fair to himself or find himself guilty. There will be no room for even-handedness.

These are the reasons why the Igbo believe strongly that no one should judge himself, his relations, in-laws and friends. It is for the same reason that close friends and relations of someone involved in a dispute are not nominated to serve as jurors in the same dispute.

There is no wrong without remedy

In Igbo, this means that *onye mefie, ka ikpe ma.* This means that only the wrongdoer who has been found guilty of an offence deserves punishment. Put simply, only the guilty deserves to be punished.

Punishment in any form is due to those who have done something wrong. It is meaningful only in response to an act or omission.

There cannot be punishment or remedy of any kind in the absence of any wrongdoing. An Igbo proverb suggests that without wrongdoing, there can be no forgiveness. *Mmefie adina, mgbayale ama di.*

Forgiveness has meaning only in terms of an act of wrongdoing. Pleas for forgiveness are credible against the background of a wrongful act or omission.

Public utility is always to be preferred to private interests

The Igbo express this sentiment simply by saying that the public – *oha* is greater than an individual member of the community: *oha ka madu.*

This is not a diminution of the worth of a person nor is it an attempt to make the individual perpetually subservient to the public. On the contrary, the Igbo recognise as well as acknowledge that there are occasions when the public good must take precedence over and above private interests.

The common good of an Igbo community is not subject to debate. It is given. It cannot be sacrificed on any altar of expediency: private or group, religious or political. An Igbo proverb explains this better: when one person cooks for the public, the food will never be enough to go round, but when an entire public cooks for one person, that person has more than he can bite, he has a problem.

In legislative, executive and judicial matters, *oha,* as the assembly of all adult male citizens, acting on behalf of everyone, is supreme. After God, *Chiukwu,* the next is *oha* and then the individual members and the groups of Igbo community. According to Okafor,

> "the supremacy of *oha,* the people's assembly over any individual or group of individuals is a living concept every Igboman deeply acknowledges. In other words, the interest of the people as a body overrides individual or sectional interest."[7]

It is difficult to imagine how justice can be achieved in a community that places individual interests over and above those of the public.

Nobody can transfer to others more rights than he has

Among the Igbo, this means that you cannot give what you do not have: *ife onye nwe ka oji eme ogo.* Put differently but with the same import, this means that in order to be kind or benevolent you do not have to steal. No one is required to steal in order to show kindness or demonstrate benevolence. To be a brother's keeper does not entail engagement in any immoral act.

To be kind or benevolent is one thing, stealing is another. The Igbo do not believe that kindness can be used to justify stealing. An act of kindness cannot be used as a justification for stealing.

---

[7] F. U. Okafor, *op. cit.,* p. 60.

To steal means to take somebody else's property secretly, and unlawfully. Stealing is morally and legally condemnable in any community. Therefore, to steal from someone in order to show kindness to another amounts to the transfer of a right that one does not have, and in this case, a precarious right.

No one may profit from his wrongdoing

This, in Igbo, is stated thus: *Onye me njo ama li ulu dina njo ome. Njo,* that is, evil, badness, wickedness, or sin, is profitable only to those who are short-sighted in the sense that they do not take a longer view of their own lives or of life in general. A wrongdoer may reap benefits from his act or omission in the short run, but in the long run, the community prevails.

The Igbo believe that the entire social bond and web of relationships may disintegrate if persons adjudged guilty are allowed to reap benefits from their own wrongdoing. Wrongdoing is certainly disruptive of the rhythm of community life. To allow persons to profit from their own wrongdoing in addition to the disruptive nature of wrongdoing is double jeopardy for a community.

A wrongdoer deserves to profit from his act or omission, negatively, in terms of the appropriate sanction – but, certainly not in a positive manner.

Analysis

These principles, as understood in Igbo, predate the Hobbesian state of nature, a hypothetical arrangement that never guaranteed the flourishing of the human species. The state of nature was characterised by chaos, violence and the war of everyone against everyone. This made life "nasty, short and brutish". The communal instinct was under-developed, unaccounted for, and was indeed negated.

These developments are necessitated by the complete, total and absolute absence of social, cultural, legal, political, and moral mechanisms for the protection, enhancement, and promotion of individual rights, privileges, liberty and freedom. There was no protection of either the public or private interests. No one was in charge of anything.

The Igbo provided the solution to the problem of political organization before the much vaunted Greek and Roman civilizations. To avoid the chaos, conflict, and disorder that arise when the affairs of human beings are left to no one or to no group of individuals, the Igbo enunciated these principles, among many others, as part of *Omenani.*

Egbe belu ugo belu, the principle of order and equity discourages intolerance, indiscretion, and disrespect for the rights of others. Human beings like the kite and eagle are enjoined by this principle to learn to accommodate, consociate, tolerate, and respect each others right, liberty and freedom.

The principle of fair hearing is meant to ensure that crooked procedures are not employed in the determination of guilt or innocence. It is intended to reduce, at least, to a tolerable degree, the natural desire or inclination for jungle justice.

Taken together, these principles, in conjunction with others, guarantee the achievement of the good life here and hereafter, as a value. This means self-realization, creative fulfilment, and joyful exuberance in accordance with the laws of the land, *iwu obodo,* as enshrined in *Omenani.*

Cumulatively, the principles help to ensure that every person is equal to the other in dignity and value. This means that each person (whether *obi,* titled men or ordinary Igbo) is equal before the law. No one, then, should be deprived of the opportunity to participate in communal life and achieve the good life for reasons unknown to *Omenani.*

The principles guarantee that persons have the freedom to select their own values, careers and life styles as long as they do not deny the same rights to others. This includes the right to privacy and non-interference but along with this is the emphasis on the development of moral education and growth in Igbo community life. This education is a communal affair primarily because the upbringing and the informal education of Igbo youth is a communal affair. Without this education the road to justice is blocked, with the attendant consequences.

These principles are endowed with the power to convince. They refer to what is evident, to public policies or to *communis consensus.* They are based on common sense, on community wisdom, or as Recasens-Siches has suggested they are based on "the logic of the reasonable"[8] Hence for Perelman, these principles "unlike

---

[8] Luis Recasens-Siches, "The Logic of the Reasonable as Differentiated from the Logic of the Rational," R.A. Newman, ed., *Essays in Jurisprudence in Honour of Roscoe Pound,* Indianapolis: Bobbs Merrill, 1962, p. 204.

demonstrative reasoning are never correct or incorrect, but either strong or weak."[9]

Igbo laws

Law in Igbo means *iwu.* This is often referred to as *iwu obodo,* that is, the law of the land, or the law of the town, or the law of the country.

From *iwu,* the following are derivable:

1. *odi na iwu:* it is forbidden by law, illegal;
2. *ti iwu:* make law or enact law;
3. *mebi iwu:* commit crime, offence, break law, sin, wrongdoing;
4. *da iwu:* to break the law.

What are these laws? Some are similar to those in the official Nigerian system while some are universal because the Igbo are part of humanity. A few are, nonetheless, distinctly Igbo. There is need to assemble them:

1. *ezune oshi:* do not steal;
2. *egbune madu:* do not kill any person;
3. *ehone:* do not commit suicide;
4. *ala na nwunye madu:* do not commit adultery;
5. *Ayi na nwunye madu oyi:* Do not flirt or befriend another person's wife;
6. *ala na nwanne-e:* do not have sex with your kith and kin – incest.
7. *ebochine madu onu:* do not slander or defame any person, don't lie or speak falsely against any person;
8. *agbana ama:* do not bear false testimony against any person or be a false witness;
9. *emena madu ife wa ama me-i:* do unto others. This is the golden rule earlier treated in this chapter;
10. *emebine ife madu ibeyi:* do not destroy or damage the property of any person. Impregnating somebody's daughter without the offer of marriage is taken as a form of destruction or damage in some communities;

---

[9] Chaim Perelman, *The New Rhetoric – A Treatise on Argumentation,* J. Wilkinson and P. Weaver, trans., Notre Dame: University Press, 1965, p. 1.

11. *anana madu ife-e n ike:* do not forcibly take over somebody's property, either real or movable.

Numbers a, b, c, j, i, and k are criminal offences regarded as *Ajo ife,* that is, that these are not just instances of wrongdoing but are instances of grievous wrongdoing. These are also moral offences.

Numbers g and h are moral offences. They can become criminal offences because of perjury.

Numbers d, e, and f are moral offences involving sex. In some communities, to commit adultery or flirt with somebody's wife is more than a moral issue. It is held that to commit adultery with any person's wife is to make an enemy out of that woman's husband.

A breach of some of these rules is regarded, not just as ordinary breach of law, but as something more than that, as something that transcends the ordinary. Such breaches are abominations: *Nso ani, or alu.*

For example, suicide is an abomination. So is murder. In both cases, apart from the prescribed sanction, the land, that is *Ani,* must be cleansed because human blood is sacred in terms of its support of life. Such blood constitutes pollutants to *Ani.* Murder and suicide are also regarded as offences against God. The reason is that God alone owns life *(Chinwendu, Chijindu),* gives life, and only God can take life. In murder and suicide, someone is attempting to oust God and thereafter play God's role.

Adultery and sexual intercourse in the afternoon and in the farmland are abominable. The values that render this sexual behaviour improper are:

1. farmland is regarded as sacred. It needs protection from defilement through sexual intercourse in the afternoon. This is taken as the most obvious and highly objectionable act of defilement;
2. the defilement will invariably make for the infertility of the farmland because the earth god and specifically the god of fertility *(ifejiokwu)* would be displeased;
3. sexual intercourse in the afternoon and in the farmland in itself debases and defiles womanhood.

These beliefs may appear irrational to the "modern mind", Igbo and non-Igbo. Yet, the beliefs have instrumental value in terms of proper and acceptable sexual behaviour among the Igbo.

Igbo laws are classifiable into two broad categories: divine and human. "There are those which might be called human laws and those whose breach is held to be, not only illegal, but also an offence against a supernatural power and particularly against *ala (Ani),* the land."[10]

Prohibitions against murder and suicide, for example, are based on divine laws. So is the prohibition against stealing. Divine laws are ordained by God, hence they are unchangeable, their demands inexorable. In contrast, the other laws are based on human reason. They are changeable and revocable. They are enacted after discussion in an assembly of adult citizens functioning in its legislative capacity. To be credible these human laws must be embedded in *Omenani.* The divine laws have long been humanized and embedded in *Omenani* because of the necessity for enforcement.

Whether divine or human, these laws are meant to serve a plurality of purposes, the most important being; (a) the protection of life and property; (b) the order, peace, justice, good management, and effective administration of public affairs in an Igbo community.

Infractions are punishable but the Igbo idea of punishment does not amount to vengeance. It is not aimed at the alienation of wrongdoers nor is it a punitive measure. It is merely to remind a wrongdoer that the part chosen is not the best. Figuratively, the offender is punished with the left hand and consoled with the right hand.

There is an interplay of rule and principle in Igbo justice system like it is in any other system. This interplay is most noticeable in the resolution of disputes.

In situations where the application of legal rules would do more harm to an extant relationship, Council normally takes refuge in the principles inherent in Igbo law. At other times, the use of principles may be the best option. These different situations are lucidly exemplified in the cases examined in detail in the next chapter.

---

[10] M. M. Green *Ibo Village Affairs,* New York: Praeger, 1964, p. 100.

Chapter 6

Justice in the resolution of conflicts

Justice and law in the context of dispute behaviour

LAW is a body of regularised procedures and normative standards considered justiciable in a given group. It contributes to the creation and prevention of disputes, and to their settlement. Justifiability is defined by Kantorwicz as the characteristic of those rules "which are considered fit to be applied by a judicial organ in some definite procedure."[1] By judicial organ Kantorowicz means "a definite authority concerned with a kind of casuistry, to wit, the application of principles to individual cases of conflict between parties."[2]

Kantorowicz uses the concept of judicial organ in a very broad sense or, as he puts it, in a very "modest and untechnical sense".[3] It includes judges, jurors, headmen, chiefs, priests, sages, council of elders, kinship tribunals, *etc.*. It is this inclusiveness and flexibility that make the concept useful in this study.

It must be emphasised from the out set that the normative standards that will be subject to analysis are applicable to a third party within a dispute context and its recognised procedures of settlement. According to Abel, "a dispute is the assertion of inconsistent claims to a resource. It is commonly justified in terms of a norm – the party or the spokesman argues that the claim ought to be satisfied."[4]

---

[1] H. Kantorowicz, *The Definition of Law*, Cambridge: University Press, 1958, p. 79.

[2] Ibid., p. 69.

[3] Ibid., p. 80.

[4] Richard L. Abel, "A Comparative Theory of Dispute Institutions in Society," *Law and*

In much the same way, Gulliver defines dispute as follows, "a dispute arises out of disagreement between persons in which the alleged rights of one party are claimed to be infringed, interfered with, or denied by the other party."[5]

Law is actualised in a dispute context in three basic ways: dispute creation, dispute prevention, and dispute settlement. These three basic ways are structurally related. Consequently, the understanding of any one of them requires the analysis of the others. To say this amount to the acknowledgement of the limitations of this chapter and perhaps, the study itself, which is mainly concerned with justice in the process of dispute settlement in Igbo culture.

For immediate purposes, it is assumed that argumentative discourse is the structured mode of actualization of law and justice in the resolution of conflicts. Legal reasoning in Igbo is dialectical and rhetorical, though the categories of reasonableness and generality are often not closed. The dialectics and rhetorics are often laced with proverbs, maxims, and anecdotes.

Dispute settlement procedure

Whenever the *Obi*-in-Council (Council) is called upon to settle a dispute, the typical procedure is as follows. The complainant goes to the palace to lodge his or her grievance.

A sheep or a goat, some kegs of palm wine and kola nuts are paid as fee to open the palace court.[6] A senior member of the council is then mandated to conduct a preliminary investigation. He will ask for the full details of the complainant's grievance in order to ascertain whether the case is of a criminal nature.[7]

Society Review, 8, 1973, pp. 226-7.

[5] Phillip Gulliver, "Introduction to Case Studies of Law in Non Western Societies," Laura Nader, ed., *Law in Culture and Society*, Chicago: Aldine, 1969, p. 14.

[6] If the complainant is the wrongdoer (as determined at the end of deliberations) the items are forfeited. If the complainant is not the wrongdoer, the other party will, as part of the settlement, return the items to the complainant. This is, in addition, to whatever fines and orders the council may decide to make.

[7] Before the advent of colonial rule, the council had jurisdiction in civil and criminal cases. The establishment of the colonial court system removed criminal matters from the jurisdiction of the council. This was achieved through government proclamation No. 5 of 1900. This drew the demarcation line.

His questions and investigation thereafter will be oriented towards establishing whether the dispute falls within the subject matters over which the council has jurisdiction. Depending on how well he knows the parties to the dispute and how much private knowledge of the dispute he already has, he will do further investigative work in order to establish the *prima facie* reasonableness of the claims in dispute.

The principles of dispute settlement are loosely applied at this stage, but this is sufficient to give the palace officials an idea or impression of the relevant features of the case, and of the norms that may apply to it.

If the council accepts to settle the dispute, as is usually the case, the defendant is notified and given a date for the determination of the rival claims. The complainant is also put on notice about the date for the hearing of his or her grievances and the determination of the claims arising therefrom. Parties to a dispute are responsible for producing their witnesses.

Where the defendant persistently absents himself or herself from the hearing, there are devices employed to ensure compliance. These are, for example, the personal intervention of the *obi,* by a friend of the defendant, by his immediate relations and the extended ones.

The parties may be accompanied to the hearing by friends, relations, and neighbours. The wife or wives, or their husbands, as the case may be, often accompany the parties to the hearing. These persons never intervene in the process of obtaining evidence from the parties. They can, at the end of the presentation of evidence and counter evidence, contribute to the discussions leading to the settlement.

The hearing is usually in an open court. Both parties and their witnesses swear to an oath. The complainant presents his or her case followed by the defendant. If there are witnesses, they are invited to testify and are cross-examined. Disputants are questioned by members of the council. Witnesses are also questioned and the parties may then engage in an exchange of views. Comments and then questions from the audience are also entertained.

Finally, three, five or seven senior members of the council including, occasionally, some persons from the audience are nominated to serve as jurors *(ume).* The jurors retire to an inner chamber to deliberate and recommend judgement to the council. In some cases, parties to a dispute are asked to excuse themselves from the deliberation in order to allow a fruitful exchange of views on the basis of the evidence presented by both sides.

From the foregoing the following points naturally emerge:

1.   The oath administered to both parties and their witnesses is tended

to enforce the morality of truth. Falsehood is culturally repugnant and condemnable;

2. Decisions through jurors *(ume)* are intended to ensure that arbitrary decisions are avoided. It is to ensure compliance with the community's standard of fairness, objectivity and truth. Justice through the jury system is dispensed by the assembly of adult citizens just as power is exercised through such an assembly;

3. Parties can object to the inclusion of persons deemed, in their opinion, to be unsuitable for jury service on the grounds of prejudice, bias or a lingering old quarrel. Any person selected for jury service can refuse without offering reasons for refusing to serve;

4. Relations and friends of both parties are normally excluded from jury service;

5. Issues not originally pleaded are not normally argued;

6. Overt mechanisms are employed to ensure that both parties do not end up as enemies, no matter the final outcome;

7. No decision is made unless both parties are heard. Not only are they heard, the complainant and the defendant are simultaneously heard in each other's presence. Their witnesses are also questioned in the presence of everyone, including the parties to a dispute.

The procedural steps prior to the hearing create an ambience of interaction and an atmosphere of evaluation which feed back upon the final stage of the process, and contribute to its outcome. The process not only reflects the jurisdiction and powers of the council but also recreates and reinforces that jurisdiction. In so doing, the decision reached is strengthened in terms of the possibility that it will be accepted by the parties to the dispute.

This is related to the problem of implementing the decision. Given the weakness of the council in terms of its lack of a coercive power similar to that in a modern state, implementation of the decision depends on its acceptance by the parties without external coercion.

Where voluntary compliance with the decision fails, the punishment, after persuasion has failed, is ostracism. In a culturally homogeneous community like the Igbo, not many persons can survive ostracism, which is intended to encourage a recalcitrant person to respect the authority of the council and the will of the community. Because of the negative impact of ostracism, parties to a dispute do recognise that non-cooperation would definitely constitute a serious problem for themselves, family members, and friends.

For a decision to be binding on parties to a dispute the following conditions must be satisfied simultaneously.

There must be voluntary submission of the dispute to the elders of the council. In complex, difficult situations, the council may not wait for this submission. Where the security of the community is concerned, the council will not bother about this submission. An example of such a situation is any abominable act: *Nso ani* - blood shed, suicide or having sex in the farmland constitute such acts.

The parties must show willingness to be bound by the decision of the council, or the freedom to reject if not satisfied.

Neither party resiles from the decision or withdraws from the entire process before the decision is reached. Such withdrawal is permissible only when all parties are in agreement to abort further proceedings, and make peace on their own.

The decision, the norms, principles and agreement that lead to it must be those enshrined in *Omenani.* The reason for this is clear. There is no crime except in accordance with the law: *Onye da iwu me njo.*

The notion of fairness

In disputes arising out of conflict of individual interests, this principle urges a real or fictitious balance of right and duties, an outcome that approximates the model of mediation. It has been suggested that we never find either pure adjudication or pure mediation in practice and that it might be more profitable to work with the categories of mixed adjudication and mixed mediation. I argue that the category of pure mediation is, indeed, a very feasible option. The rhetorical needs of the argument may lead the dispute settler to present a decision as a compromise as is often the case in Igbo judicial ideology, called *Iha enye nkaku.* This can be illustrated by the analysis of the following case examples.

Case No. 1

Mr. Maidor[8] sold a part of his cassava plot to Mr. Okolie for ₦500. The

---

[8] All the names used in these examples are fictitious. The cases examined and analysed are real which the author witnessed for the purposes of this study. The cases were taken

purchaser paid one quarter of the price immediately and promised to pay the balance in three instalments. On the date agreed, he paid the first instalment. The second instalment was also paid on time. However, instead of giving the money to the seller himself, Mr. Okolie gave it to the seller's wife. She spent the money at her pleasure without telling her husband. Besides, she was unfaithful to her husband and had gone to bed with the purchaser's brother. On hearing this, the seller, Mr. Maidor, sent his wife away and demanded repossession of the remaining cassava plot. Mr. Okolie, the purchaser, complained that he had duly paid the instalment and intended to pay the final instalment. He had given the second instalment to the woman in the belief that she would give it to her husband. He then took the matter to the Obi-in-Council for determination and settlement.

The *Obi*-in-Council said that it would not be fair to revoke the sale since the purchaser had acted in good faith throughout. On the other hand, the seller should not be injured by the purchaser's failure to give the money directly to him. Therefore, the instalment in question should not be credited to the balance of the price. The *Obi*-in-Council finally decided, and the parties agreed, that the purchaser should pay the instalment as originally agreed upon beginning from the ill-fated second one, while the revocation as requested by the seller should not be allowed.

The Obi-in-Council knew the dramatic circumstances of this case, because palace officials had a pre-understanding of the facts and norms involved in the dispute. In demanding repossession of the cassava plot Mr. Maidor was using Mr. Okolie as a scapegoat for his anger at Mr. Okolie's brother. But it was clear that Mr. Okolie had not been involved in his brother's affairs with Mr. Maidor's wife, and had acted in good faith.

After the parties presented their cases, palace officials used the principle of fairness to eliminate some extreme solutions, thus creating the normative ground upon which a middle-of-the-road decision could gradually be shaped. Palace officials believed that Mr. Okolie had conducted himself as a reasonable, reliable purchaser. He paid the instalment on time. The fact that he made one of the payments to Mrs. Maidor cannot be taken as a violation of the contract. Since Mr. and Mrs. Maidor are married, the cassava plot is the property of both, what belongs to one belongs to both. Mr. Okolie gave the money to Mrs. Maidor reasonably assuming and believing that she would give the money to the husband. Consequently, it would be unfair to give no

---

from the palaces of the Obi in Aniocha north local government area.

consideration to the legitimate interests of Mr. Okolie by revoking the sale of the cassava. It would be unfair to give no consideration to Mr. Maidor's legitimate interest in obtaining full payment for his cassava. By excluding two alternatives that totally sacrifice the interests of one party, the Obi-in-Council legitimated, indeed necessitated, a decision that would make for balance. Mr. Okolie will retain the cassava plot but the payment of the second instalment would be repeated. Mr. Maidor will not repossess the cassava but would receive the full payment originally agreed upon.

It is interesting to note that the *Obi*-in-council avoids any involvement in the sexual issues that gave rise to the dispute. The object of the dispute is strictly maintained within the defined boundaries of the law of contract even though palace officials knew that Mr. Maidor was using Mr. Okolie as a scapegoat for his brother. I think that the conciliatory decision which, on the surface of the legal discourse, appeared as the normative result of the exclusion of extreme alternatives, was motivated by the Council's policy of minimising antagonism and hatred between litigants. The *Obi*-in-council may have been particularly anxious to persuade the parties to accept the mediation as a fair settlement of the processed dispute because this might settle the real dispute without explicit argumentation. If this is the case, then, the processed and the real dispute, that is adultery, was intentionally kept separate in order to allow an economical settlement of both.

Case No. 2

The decision in this second case has many things in common with the first one. Miss Dike was in senior secondary form one when she was impregnated by her boy friend, Master Okoh. Mr. Dike was so incensed by his daughter's behaviour that he drove her away from home, vowing never to pay school fees for her any more. Her behaviour had brought shame and ridicule to her family. Master Okoh's family accepted the responsibility but Miss Dike lost her baby after the delivery. Upon this development, Okoh's family reversed their earlier decision. They then promptly asked Miss Dike to return to her family. But her parents would not give her shelter or food. And because of the aforementioned, Miss Dike took her case to the *Obi*-in-Council.

Akin to the previous example, a lot of spadework was done behind closed doors in order to find and establish a common ground between the parties to the dispute. The Obi-in-council blamed the two youngsters for bringing shame, ridicule and suffering to their families.

It then decided, upon agreement by the parties, that it would be unfair to Mr. Dike to hold that Okoh's family has no more responsibility towards Miss Dike. It ordered that Okoh's family should find a suitable school for Miss Dike to enable her continue her studies. In addition, they should also pay her school fees for one year to enable her complete her SS 1. Mr. Dike was, on the other hand, prevailed upon to take over, thereafter, the payment to enable her daughter complete her secondary education.

It is interesting to note that nothing about marriage between Miss Dike and Master Okoh was discussed. It was not, simply, because it was not the issue. Far more relevant, however, is how the notion of fairness has been given expression but in conciliatory and non-adversary tones.

Case No. 3

Chief Osu and Mr. Oseji disagreed over the method to be adopted in sharing kolanuts at the meeting of blacksmiths *(otu uzu)*. Both had been admitted as new members after their performance of the traditional rites and ceremonies. Osu, a chief, wanted the sharing to take cognizance of his standing in the village. He is, after all, a chief. Oseji, on his part, wanted the sharing to be along age-grade system, that is, the eldest takes his share first. In terms of the age-long practice and custom among the blacksmiths, both were wrong in their contentions. But both men were impatient. Before the final decision by their fellow blacksmiths, they left the meeting swearing, cursing and accusing one another.

Every member, however, knew that the matter had not been settled. It was not surprising, therefore, that a day after, the wives of both men fought in the market place. The women tore their clothing into shreds in public, whereupon, the matter went to the *Obi*-in-Council for settlement.

The leadership of the blacksmiths were invited. Statements were made and countered. At the end, the *Obi*-in-Council decided thus:

1. the initial positions of both men were wrong following the submission from the leader of the blacksmiths' association;
2. both were blamed for their impatience;
3. Oseji was blamed for his non-recognition of Osu's position in the

village;

4.   Osu was equally blamed for his arrogance;

5.   Osu's wife, who started the fight in the market place, was blamed for taking the law into her own hands, as it was clear that she never acted on instructions from her husband;

6.   Oseji's wife was also blamed for not exercising some restraint.

What is significant here is that the *Obi*-in-Council did not have to take over the responsibilities of blacksmith's association, hence the prior invitation to their leaders. There is an element of "give and take" in the decision. Both men lost as well as gained something resulting from the decision. As in the other example, the sole intention is not to encourage acrimonious relation-ships but to ensure that at the end of the settlement litigants are fraternal and are their brother's keepers again.

Case No. 4

The plaintiff, Mrs. Okolo and her four children returned home from Kano after one of those deadly Maitatsine Moslem religious riots. Mr. Okolo was killed during the riots.

At the same time, Miss Okojie, the defendant came to the plaintiff with her two children saying she had been sleeping on the street with her children because she had no place to live. Miss Okojie who lost her immediate family during the civil war, knew that a small house was vacant in Mrs. Okolo's compound. She pleaded for assistance and to be allowed to move into the said house.

Compassionately, Mrs. Okolo agreed and even allowed Miss Okojie the use of the furniture in the small house. Mrs. Okolo did not charge rent and therefore got none.

Some eighteen months after, Mrs. Okolo wanted the small house back because her sister with three children, whose husband died in a motor accident, was returning home and had no place to live. Miss Okojie refused to leave.

The Council listened to both parties. Miss Okojie acknowledged the help she received from Mrs. Okolo but argued that she could not leave the house because she had no place to go. She claimed she had no money to pay rent. And with two children, it was unlikely anybody will rent a house or room to her, without paying some rent.

Mrs. Okolo stated in her reply that Miss Okojie could afford to pay rent, being a prostitute who makes money. Miss Okojie denied this accusation. She rhetorically asked Mrs. Okolo whether she herself was not hawking her body too.

The Council after deliberations, asked Miss Okojie to find a room because she, in fact, had not tried to do so at all. She was reminded of the kind gesture and the hand of fellowship extended to her by Mrs. Okolo. She was told that her lack of co-operation was not fair.

Mrs. Okolo's sister and children needed a place to live. It was reasonable that Mrs. Okolo wanted to help her sister and the children. She had a greater responsibility to help them than anyone else including Miss Okojie. On the basis of these reasons, Miss Okojie was given four weeks to find accommodation and leave the small house in Mrs. Okolo's compound. Miss Okojie agreed to this reluctantly, while Mrs. Okolo was also persuaded to accept.

This case is characterised by normative consensus between the parties especially in relation to property law. Mrs. Okolo granted Miss Okojie a precarious tenancy because she had the legal right (as well as moral) to repossess the small house. These legal conclusions were not questioned by Miss Okojie because they were non-issues.

The presentation and argumentation of both parties lacked legal tone on account of this. This exchange was predominantly moral. The parties accepted the same normative principle: need for shelter but this same principle was used to advance contradictory claims.

Both parties attempted to describe facts in such a way that individual claims appear morally superior to the other. Mrs. Okolo laid emphasis on her moral integrity in terms of her compassionate treatment of Miss Okojie: free house, free use of furniture and no rent was demanded. Only compelling need forced her to ask Miss Okojie to find an alternative accommodation.

On her part, Miss Okojie tried to show why she couldn't leave. She tried to demonstrate that she was not an ingrate but that her condition was desperate: she had no place to live and had no money to pay rent. She consciously pushed the argument of necessity to its most extreme level.

The emotional exchange between both enabled the council to come to one indubitable conclusion, that is, that there was another dispute, which was not before them. The dispute over the small house was the superficial conflict between both women. The settlement was restricted to the issue of the small house and argumentative strategy was organised around this issue.

On moral grounds, the moral claims of both parties seemed to even out; to a tie score: the need for shelter applied to both. On legal grounds however, Mrs. Okolo definitely edged out Miss Okojie because she never disputed Mrs. Okolo's ownership and right to repossession.

From the foregoing, it is clear that the council decided this case on legal grounds but presented the decision not on legal terms because (a) the parties chose moral arguments and (b) the principle of fairness and of co-operation was used to exclude an evidently unfair alternative decision. The main problem posed for council was not merely that of the balance of interests but predominantly that of the conflict of moral duties.

Why was the council silent on the real dispute that was behind this case? There is a principle among the Igbo of Aniocha north which insists that you normally base decision or judgement *only* on what parties to a dispute have said in each other's presence, and in an open court: *ife wa kpenye onye ka oha.* You do not invent dispute for people. No one has a right to do this.

Hence, in the final settlement, the council was careful to concentrate on the issue of the small house, consciously downplaying and omitting the other facts that the parties had asserted. During the preliminary investigation carried out by palace officials, it was unearthed that the real dispute was about a man. Both women were fighting for the love of a man but they never disclosed this. They merely alluded to it by the use of stigma and counter stigma. The council showed no interest because neither party was interested in processing it for settlement.

Finally, in case three, the notion for fairness was subtly used to arrive at a mediated decision. However, in the present instance, that is, case four, mediation does not appear to have had a focal place. Miss Okojie lost her case even though she was allowed to stay in the small house for another month. Yet, it was also very obvious that the council was re-engineering a shattered relationship by persuading both parties to cool off together for another month.

Case No. 5

According to Mr. Agaju, he bought a part of Mr. Emordi's rafia palm plantation for the purpose of tapping rafia palm wine. He paid ₦100 and had put his younger brother in-charge. His younger brother worked on the plantation for nineteen months and left.

Now, Mr. Emordi wants to sell the entire plantation but Mr. Agaju would not agree because according to him he owns a part of the plantation. If there was going to be any sale, he would decide when and how to do so.

Mr. Emordi denied that he sold a part of his plantation to Mr. Agaju or to any one else. He allowed Mr. Agaju the use of a part of his plantation because (a) he was not tapping wine in the whole plantation (b) Mr. Agaju expressed real need for assistance because he was financially distressed at that point in time.

Mr. Agaju stated further that there were witnesses to the sale but upon request from the council that he produce a document attesting the sale, he declined on the grounds that Mr. Emordi refused to issue a receipt. When asked to produce his witnesses, he mentioned names but after three adjournments, none of his witnesses came to testify.

The council, after listening to both parties, summarised and decided as follows:

a) Witnesses or document or both attesting to the sale would have been helpful but were not presented;
b) Council restated its neutrality as always;
c) It said it had no reason to doubt any of the parties; and
d) That it is interested only in finding a fair solution.

To find that fair solution, it made the following suppositions:

a) Let's suppose that Mr. Agaju paid ₦100 for the nineteen months his younger brother tapped wine from the plantation.
b) Let's further suppose that Mr. Emordi gives the ₦100 back. In that case Mr. Agaju would have to pay the rent or royalty for the period in question, that is, nineteen months.
c) Let's again further suppose that the rent or royalty is fixed at ₦10.00 per month. For nineteen months that amounts to ₦190. Now, Mr. Agaju paid only ₦100, this means that he still owed Mr. Emordi the sum of ₦90.
d) Against this background, it would be fair, council reasoned, that Mr. Agaju forgets the ₦100 he paid. In that case Mr. Emordi will also forget the ₦90 owed him.
e) As a matter of fact, Mr. Agaju may have paid the ₦100 but his younger brother tapped wine in that plantation for nineteen months.

The council on the basis of these suppositions and reasoning proposed a compromise solution. Mr. Agaju will forget the payment he claimed to have made and Mr. Emordi will have to forget the rent.

This case is an example of where the principle of fairness has been used to reach an outcome of false mediation. This means the decision is presented as mediation but is implicitly adjudicative in nature.

Without stating it explicitly in very clear terms, the council was engaged in adjudication. The legal norms involved are the formal rule requiring a written document to certify the sale of part of the plantation and the substantive rules of property law. The real dispute is about the legal title to a part of the plantation.

Mr. Emordi contended that he owned the whole of the plantation and had the right to dispose of it according to his wishes any time. Mr. Agaju, a precarious possessor, contended that he bought a part of the plantation, and that part could not be sold without his consent.

In support of his claims, Mr. Agaju resorted to formal argument, and asserted that he had witnesses to testify to the deal. He back-pedalled when he could present neither document nor witnesses in support of his position.

The council refused to follow Mr. Agaju in that formalist path, a path that is highly inappropriate to an argument based on fairness and cooperation.

Instead, council ingeniously presented an argument in which a decision against one of the parties is subtly regarded as a compromise between them. To achieve this, council changed the object to the dispute through the subtle manipulation of the reality of the situation: Let's suppose…

The logic of the situation was inverted in order to achieve an intended end. This was done by transposing a dispute over the sale of property into a dispute over the amount of rent or royalty. Reality is reconstructed in such a way as to make it appear that Mr. Agaju owed Mr. Emordi some money. To achieve this, council separated the ₦100 from the legal situation that prompted it. Instead, the amount is transformed from the total payment of the purchase price into partial payment of rent or royalty with the conclusion that even at that the rent or royalty was low.

The council decided against Mr. Agaju on substantive grounds, with the aid of assumptions of what a person of reasonable, practical judgement and endowed with native intelligence would do – the reasonable price, rent or royalty expected from such a person. The argument presented by council reflects, in an inverted form, the process through which the decision was reached.

Case No. 6

There are two kinds of land tenure area in Aniocha north local government area:

a) the family owned land; and
b) the community owned land.

Family land is meant for residence only, and is not subject to the vagaries of the market. Community land is for farming. The inhabitants recognise two kinds of farm work:

i) shifting cultivation which does not involve individual ownership of farm land. Besides, it is mandatory that economic crops and trees are not planted;
ii) farming that involves economic crops as done in plantations.

No one is allowed to plant economic crops in the community-owned farmland. Besides, it is known that the cassava plant is ready for harvest from one to three years depending on the particular species. The community repossesses a particular farmland after three years. At the expiration of this period of time any other member of the community has a right to farm on the same land bearing the same conditions in mind.

This was the situation (remains the same now) when Mr. Bolu prepared a portion of land for farming activities. During the farming period, he did not only cultivate yam and cassava, he also cultivated economic trees. He planted rubber trees and turned a part of the same farm land into a plantain plantation.

Shortly after these developments became public, the town progressive union, a community development agency, tried unsuccessfully to persuade Mr. Bolu to cut the trees.

The council waded into the matter and ordered Mr. Bolu to cut the rubber trees himself or alternatively engage some other people to do so. When it became clear that Mr. Bolu was ready to do neither, the council ordered all able bodied men on a Monday morning to do the cutting. This was successfully done.

Mr. Bolu sued the entire town at the customary court and lost. This illustrates the collective (public) interest overriding a claim of individual title, a precarious title as in this case. It shows how and why public interest takes precedence over that of a private, individual member. For it is the community that permits the possibility of peaceful, decent and upright social life.

Igbo law deals with private interests in much the same way as the official Nigerian law. This similarity comes through the inversion of the basic norm that allows Igbo law and Nigerian law to provide similar normative solutions to similar problems.

It is clear, however, that this similarity does not extend to technical details but remains at the level of a broad normative outlook.

Case No. 7

Adafor and Adaolie, both women, are friends. Adaolie is a widow. Adafor is still happily married.

Both women went to their cassava farms, uprooted cassava, and put them separately in the stream for fermentation. Both women have corners in the stream that share a boundary made of stones, pebbles, and logs of wood. Every adult woman in the community has a corner *(uno akpu)* to herself in the stream where cassava roots are kept for some days to enable them ferment.

Okoh, a twenty year old, and eldest son of Adafor went to Adaolie's corner in the steam and stole her fermented cassava. He also stole from his mother's corner. Some women saw Okoh, on the day of the theft, with cassava but thought his mother solicited his assistance.

Okoh's mother did know of this theft but did not associate any of her children with it. She informed Adaolie, her friend, of the theft. On investigation, both women found that Okoh was seen preparing fermented cassava in the steam some days earlier. When Okoh was confronted with this allegation he denied it in very strong terms.

Both women, particularly Adafor, mother of the suspect, decided to forget the matter. Both found consolation in the adage which says that the victim of theft is better, at least, in material terms than the thief.

A few days later, Adaolie, on stronger evidence, came and confronted Okoh, not only with the allegation, but with the names of women who saw him in the stream preparing fermented cassava. When Okoh continued to deny, Adaolie informed her friend Adafor (mother of Okoh) that she was taking the matter to the Police.

Okoh, at twenty, was preparing for his age-grade initiation ceremony. A matter of this nature, if allowed to explode, meant that (a) Okoh's initiation might be postponed indefinitely, (b) there will be loss of pride, respect, and credibility among age-mates and peers, (c) the ceremony, whenever it is done, would have lost the aura, mystic and lustre that are part of it.

Against this background, Okoh's parents went to work on Adaolie, her other friends, elders of her late husband's family and her parents. The intention was to prevent a scandal through a subtle damage control measure.

These mediative efforts were on, largely unconcretized yet, when Adaolie was returning from the evening market and met Okoh beating Eke, a young girl of ten. By the time Adaolie arrived at the scene, Okoh had torn Eke's blouse and brassiere. Eke was half nude. Adaolie intervened, pleaded with Okoh to no avail and then tried to take Eke away. Okoh reacted violently to her efforts. In the process, he pushed Adaolie down. Her wares, particularly oil, salt and kerosene spilled over and got mixed with sand. She lost the sum of ₦200 (two hundred naira) in the confusion that ensued.

Her late husband's family concluded that they have had enough. They thus instructed Adaolie to take the case to the council rather than the Police. She did.

Most members of the council were familiar with the main outlines of the case. Both were, as usual, invited and heard. To make matters worse, Okoh relentlessly continued to deny the allegations. Against this background, council asked him to take oath (a kind of modern day lie dictator). Okoh initially agreed but later on refused.

His refusal meant only one thing: that he stole the cassava belonging to Adaolie and subsequently lied about it. The truth about the theft had an effect. It enabled the council to take over the mediative efforts earlier started by Okoh's family. Besides, the council decided that:

a) Okoh should give two head-pans of cassava to Adaolie instead of one head pan which he stole. The reason for this was that Adaolie, being a widow, needed assistance from members of the community;
b) Okoh should pay for the wares destroyed when he pushed Adaolie down on her intervention the day he beat Eke. He should refund the missing ₦200;
c) He should pay for the blouse and brassiere he tore when he beat up Eke;
d) His initiation ceremony into age-grade was postponed for thirteen moons, which is the equivalent of an Igbo year;
e) He should, every morning and evening, for five days, use a gong to announce to the community that he stole Adaolie's cassava from her corner in the stream, and that he lied when he denied the allegation.

He should plead for forgiveness from the community, particularly from Adaolie. He should promise that he would never molest the kids in the community. He should finally announce that he would never again steal, lie or molest kids;

f) Okoh's parents were assured of council supportive role whenever they decided to go to Eke's parents and Adaolie's families for the customary "thank you" visit;

g) The council finally insisted that Okoh should comply with all that has been decided. It gave him seven days to do so. It warned that in the event of non-compliance and in the absence of good reasons for not doing so during the period stipulated, Adaolie should invite the Police, with the council firmly behind her;

h) These measures were necessary, council reasoned, in order to put a stop to the kind of behaviour exhibited by Okoh;

i) The council thanked Adaolie for her patience and display of maturity. It equally thanked Okoh's parents for embarking on the resolution of the problem before their son made nonsense of their efforts.

This was a clear case of theft and physical assault: theft of Adaolie's cassava and physical assault on Eke and Adaolie.

This case was decided on *quasi*-legal grounds but disguised as mediation. Mediation did not occupy a central position in the process of decision making because the council, in a subtle manner, adjudicated. Okoh lost the case not only because the facts in his favour were not weighty enough but because he was wrong. A wrongdoer deserves punishment.

By asking Okoh to make restitution for the stolen cassava and to double the quantity to be returned, council was making an attempt to deter others. By asking Okoh to make reparations to those he injured psychologically, council was trying to assuage the harm already done.

Case No. 8

This case involved Dube and Ike, two sixteen year olds in senior secondary school class one. Both conspired and stole planks from Ene and Eze, respectively. Ene and Eze were building houses and had sewn logs of wood for that purpose.

Ene did not know of the theft. Eze discovered the theft when he went to Uzo, a carpenter, to find out when work would commence on the roofing of his house. In the carpenter's workshop he saw a table made with fresh *iroko* wood. His own planks were sewn from *iroko* wood.

On inquiry, Uzo said Ike brought the wood for the tables. On further examination Eze found other planks sewn from *obeche* wood. He remembered that Ene's planks were sewn from *obeche* wood. When he got home, he drew Ene's attention to what he found in the carpenter's workshop. When Ene checked his stock he found that some planks were, indeed, missing. Both went back to the carpenter to ascertain the actual state of affairs. The carpenter restated his earlier claim before both men to the effect that Ike brought the woods (*iroko* and *obeche* types) to him for making tables for sale.

Before both men left the workshop, the carpenter told them that he had informed Ike of Eze's complaint that the planks sewn from *iroko* wood were stolen from his stock.

Ike, on his part alerted Dube of the impending trouble. He told Dube that he could not take the heat from the two men. He would own up the theft of Eze's wood. He asked Dube to do the same or he (Ike) would tell the truth concerning both thefts. Dube did not like this.

Dube in an apparent attempt to cover up the theft, begged Dilim, a twenty-seven year old man, to claim that he (Dilim) sold the wood to him.

When Eze and Ene met Ike, Ike apologized for the theft, pleaded for forgiveness and promised to return the unused wood and the table to Eze. On Ene's wood, he directed them to talk to Dube. When the men met Dube, he agreed that he took planks of *obeche* wood to Uzo, the carpenter, for making tables. He claimed that Dilim sold the wood to him.

On agreement the three: Eze, Ene, and Dube went to Dilim who not only claimed but vigorously insisted that he sold the wood to Dube. However, on further discussion, Eze and Ene found that Dilim gave no satisfactory answers. Dissatisfied with Dilim, Ene took his case to the council.

At the council, all parties were, as usual, present. Two things bothered the council:

a) Dilim's insistent claim that he sold wood to Dube, when it was clear from investigation that Dilim had never sewn wood;

b) it was also found that Ike could not make good his promise to tell the truth because Dilim had threatened him..

Council's only recourse to Dilim's claim was oath taking in its most severe form. Dilim agreed to this but on the day set aside for it, he changed his mind. He admitted he did not sell wood to Dube or to any one else. He admitted he lied when he made that claim but that he did so in order to protect Dube. He admitted that he threatened Ike for the same purpose.

The council, after weighing the pros and cons and with the consent of all parties, took the following decisions.

The unused planks and the tables made from them were to be returned to their owners. Dube and Ike were severely rebuked for indulging in such negative acts instead of studying hard and assisting their parents in the farm. The village musicians who normally compose songs for annual festivals were implored to compose songs with the misdeeds of Dube and Ike. The purpose of making music and satirical songs with their names was to ridicule and thereafter reintegrate them. Their parents were praised for their assistance in finding the truth, and in exposing wrongdoing instead of covering it up.

Uzo, the carpenter, was praised for telling the truth. The council said it was particularly pleased that the carpenter never, at any time, reneged from the truth. It reasoned that if Uzo had not opened up, right from the outset, the truth about the thefts would never have been known.

The council said it was very displeased with the role played by Dilim in the matter. The council argued that:

a) To hide the truth is against the ethos of the community;
b) To hide a wrong doer means that either Dilim is a thief, was the brain behind the thefts or both;
c) And that these acts of omission were unbecoming of a man of Dilim's age.

For encouraging theft and for preventing the detection of theft by lieing, Dilim was,

a) Fined seven goats and given twenty one days to pay;
b) He was to use the gong to announce every morning and evening to the community, for five days, that he lied when he said that he sold wood to Dube; that he would neither hide wrongdoers nor lie again; and plead for forgiveness. Dilim had to tell the community that his claims were utterly spurious.

The council threatened that in the event of Dilim not complying with its decision, it would itself invite the police. It further threatened that in the event of an invitation being extended to the police, the council would protect the sixteen-year-olds. It would inform the police that Dilim actually stole the planks.

During the preliminary investigation by palace officials, it was found that there has been a long standing misunderstanding between Dilim and Ene, the details of which were very sketchy. It was known that both did not enjoy each others company. It was clear, therefore, that Dilim was protecting Dube, and lied, in order to hurt Ene the more.

But this long-standing dispute was neither before the council nor alluded to by either of the two men. Yet, the council thought it fit to indirectly refer to it. The council warned all the parties to the dispute that it is an offence against the ancestors, the earth goddess, and the almighty God for a brother to nurse ill feelings against another brother, and this for a long time. Left unburdened, it could lead to the death of the person engaged in it.

This was a case of theft that involved two juveniles and an adult who was bent on a revenge mission even when the opportunity for such a mission was most inauspicious and criminal.

The council decision was a mixture of adjudication and mediation. Dube, Ike and Dilim lost, and were punished for their individual roles. The threat of police invitation for non-compliance, by the council, was intended to serve two purposes:

a) To ensure compliance on the part of Dilim; and
b) To remind and warn members of the community that, that kind of behaviour is most unacceptable.

This case, like that of number 7, also illustrates how the threat of police intervention is invoked in tandem with the official law of Nigeria.

The peace sermon at the end of the deliberations was intended to persuade Dilim and Ene to make conciliatory moves to each other or for both to forget their misunderstanding.

The decision, on the whole, showed that Igbo judicial system has provision for the management of juvenile offenders. To make music with the names of Dube and Ike, and with their criminal conduct may be regarded as mild in comparison with their offences, but it was clear from council deliberations that while it was insistent on punishing them, it was equally interested in their future. The council may have drawn support from Igbo proverb which says that only fools will scratch their bodies to the extent of drawing blood, and thus sore.

An analysis of the argument of the council in support of its sanctions on Dilim showed that he was treated, and rightly too, as an accomplice or as an accessory to the crime of theft. Even if he was not, a position not supported by the evidence, the council's interpretation was consistent with Dilim's behaviour.

Both cases (seven and eight) share a common factual origin in terms of being theft. In both cases, the council insisted on restitution and reparation. From the point of view of Igbo customary law, stealing is reprehensible and punishable. Legal title to stolen property is precarious. The sources of legal precariousness are irrelevant to the status of such titles under Igbo customary law. This normative ground is shared with the official Nigerian law.

Case No. 9

The case illustrated the problem and issues in Igbo customary family law and sexual morality.

Ejime and Ada have been married for ten years with three children. Ada is hot tempered and an extrovert, while Ejime, the husband, is an introvert. But this was no reason for the problem in their union.

However, they quarrelled often, cursed quite often, shouted at each other and on rare occasions, Ejime beat his wife. Their neighbours got tired of them. Some of them stopped bothering about the couple whenever they were known to have started their usual quarrels. They reconciled as often as they quarrelled.

During one of their quarrels, both of them crossed the normative rubicon in respect of the moral standards expected to be maintained by married men and women. There are certain things (speech, behaviour, etc.) expected of, and from married men and women.

On this occasion, Ejime and Ada did not just curse themselves or their parents as was usually the case with them, they used abominable, indecent and foul language on each other. They cursed each other with their sexual organs. For Ada, Ejime must meet his end through her virgina, while for Ejime, Ada must be suffocated with his penis.

Sexual offences and other offences concerning the womenfolk are the responsibility of the *omu* association of women headed by the *omu*, the leader of the women folk. The couple were invited by the association, not really for a hearing but to remind them of the extant rule in respect of their behaviour. In this case, the couple was heard but this changed nothing.

The sanction for what they did and said to each other is well known. Ada was to be escorted out of the community until such a time that she can perform the cleansing ceremonies. Until then, she cannot return to her house and her husband. Ejime, on his part, has no peace, cannot attend any meeting until he performed the prescribed ceremonies.

The *omu* association held that the couple, with their statements, polluted the body of each other. They devalued each other in the process. They polluted the earth and its gods. For these reasons, both cannot sleep together, cannot touch each other, cannot do anything together as husband and wife until the cleansings were done and fines paid to *omu* association.

Sexual morality is strict and rigorously enforced. One of the reasons for this fact is that divorce is as possible as passing the head of a cow through the eye of a needle. Neighbours, friends, distant and immediate relations are as interested in the success of a marriage as the couple themselves. So also is the interest in preventing a divorce on the ground that the welfare of the children overrides. Even where there are no children, couples are encouraged to stay and live together. In particular, the woman is reminded that an unmarried woman is a nuisance of some sort in the community. Marriage is a status conferring mechanism which an unmarried woman needs but does not have, and cannot have while single.

The institution of the family is protected and defended collectively through the observance of certain normative standards in behaviour and speech. These standards are required if the family is to continue to play its role as a primary agent of socialization.

The arguments are morally hinged. They are based on the perceived survival needs of the community. The reasons adduced for the views taken by the *omu* association are meant to remind the couple of their position as role models for their children and others in the community.

Case No. 10

There are two types of land tenure recognised by Igbo customary land law: family and communal land. No one is allowed to build on communal land. Private houses are built on family land.

Mr. Nwaka, during the construction of his house, extended one of the walls so much so that the street, already very narrow, was almost completely obstructed. Some neighbours complained to Nwaka who simply ignored them. Some elders, based on the complaint of the neighbours of Nwaka, inspected the extension and concluded that the street has been virtually closed to traffic by the construction. They met Nwaka and explained the situation to him. Again, Nwaka ignored their explanation and pleas for a reconsideration of the extended walls of his house.

The elders took the matter to the council. Palace officials inspected the extension and had an audience with Nwaka where the matter was discussed. Nwaka was reluctant to do any thing about it but the palace officials pushed the matter very hard.

The officials argued that if someone died, the coffin could not pass down the street. Those riding bicycles, motor cyclists, and pedestrians would have problems of easy passage on that spot. Faced with the refusal of Nwaka to co-operate, the officials warned him of the consequences of his selfish and unreasonable behaviour. They threatened to demolish the unlawful extension on the grounds that the council, on behalf of the community, had the right to do so. The palace officials left without Nwaka making any commitment.

Shortly after the officials had left, Nwaka demolished the wall himself, with the extension.

Nwaka's defence at each of the levels of discourse were that:

a) the street had always been narrow;
b) he had not extended the original dimensions of his house (legal discourse); and
c) he had invested money in the construction of the wall and had neither money nor time to demolish and reconstruct it again (moral discourse and discourse of necessity).

It was clear to palace officials that what Nwaka did was a flagrant violation of Igbo norm that elevates communal interest over and above private ones. The street was virtually closed by Nwaka's construction. This denied neighbours and other people access to the main street.

The normative needs of the factual situation were so evident, yet, palace officials thought it necessary to discuss with Nwaka. By representing the interest of the community, the council functioned either as a judicial body or as an administrative agency or both.

Since Nwaka showed no respect for the norm he had violated, palace officials turned to the *(topos)* principle of a reasonable citizen. By discounting the interests of his neighbours he was unreasonable because if everyone behaved like him it would be impossible to live in the community.

His co-operation was requested and required and in the circumstances the emphasis on co-operation was transformed into a rhetorical principle put at the service of reinforcing the principle of a reasonable citizen: a reasonable citizen not only does not violate communal interests but cooperates to restore them when they have been violated.

In the course of their discussion with Nwaka, palace officials managed to magnify the unreasonableness of Nwaka's behaviour by rhetorically expanding the object of the dispute.

a) Nwaka's conflict was not only with those who live on the street but also those who died in the town whose coffins had to pass through the street on their way to their burial places;
b) To be disrespectful to the dead is a heinous moral offence in the community. Nwaka was therefore violating the interests of the living and the dead;
c) Nwaka's offence extended beyond the neighbourhood because it damaged the collective interest in the cleanliness of the environment;
d) The construction violated the community interest in free passage through the street; and
e) The construction is, therefore, forbidden because it is detrimental to communal interests.

Nwaka was not persuaded with the argument based on co-operation because he had invested too much on the extension of his wall. When therefore, it became obvious to palace officials that they were heading to nowhere with Nwaka, they resorted to threat and intimidation. In Igbo customary law, intimidation and co-operation would appear to be dialectically apposite

Intimidation became an option only after the reasonable decision or refusal of a citizen to co-operate has been established. Once intimidation was resorted to, the legal discourse changed direction.

Nwaka's conduct violated Igbo law of community interest as well as the official law of Nigeria that forbids (and orders the demolition of) unauthorized, illegal structures of any sort. As long as the principle of co-operation dominated the arguments, palace officials emphasised the Igbo norm. When they turned to threat and intimidation, they subtly relied on the laws of Nigeria.

This is an example of where an official Nigeria law is invoked to protect the recognised interest of a community. It is also an example of a situation where a legal title or claim is rejected because the public interest is at stake.

Mediation and consensus

From the ten case studies analysed in the preceding subsection, the importance of decisions reached through consensus was highlighted. Behind the idea of arriving at decisions acceptable to both sides through consensus, is the notion of mediation. Mediation is the dominant model of dispute settlement in Igbo culture so much so that adjudication is disguised as mediation. The customary judicial process among the Igbo resolves around mediation. There is always the desire to reach a compromise in which each party will give something and get something in return (see diagram 4, p.177).

In this respect, Igbo law *(iwu obodo)* differs from the official Nigeria legal system in which the model of adjudication (all-or-nothing decisions) prevail, although the extent of the difference may often be exaggerated. In each of the examples analysed, no explicit adjudicative process took place. The council, though entirely neutral, never saw itself as an adjudicator. It saw itself as a mediator trying to bring two warring parties together.

The predominance of mediation in a given situation may be due to several factors. It is a reflection of much broader cultural postulates. It may be related to the type of social relations between the parties to a dispute. It may result from the fact that the palace lacks the power to impose its decision. Granted all these factors, it appears that the overriding aim of mediation is the restoration and preservation of relationships.

Given the nature and style of Igbo community life, street orientation, face-to-face relationship, gossiping, mutual gifts of use values in knowledge and skills, neighbours, friends and relatives are frequently involved in dispute prevention and settlement. Since the palace has no formal power of sanction and has no enforcement agency similar to the modern police, mediation is a far more useful reinforcing mechanism. Threats in the form of ostracism are used when necessary but the sanction is only intended to enforce compliance not to alienate. These factors are mere pre-conditions.

Mediation occurs through rhetoric which creates the orientation towards consensus upon which the mediator builds. Consensus, not dissensus, is the end product of mediation, whereas dissensus and the imposition of decisions, not consensus, are the end products of adjudication. Adjudication and mediation may, in their separate ways, arrive at justice but while mediation aims at reconciliation, adjudication has little or no room for that.

In modern Nigeria, Igbo community is just a part, yet, its internal legality shares some of the characteristics of the legal process in Nigeria. The legal tools in Igbo communities remain amenable for use in a wider social context. For example, wide distribution of legal skills as expressed in the absence of professionalism, manageable and autonomous institutions as expressed in easy accessibility and participation, non-coercive justice as expressed in both the absence of professionalism and the orientation towards consensus.[9]

Consensus may well be related to conflict at the different levels of belief and behaviour. The distinction is between; (a) the community level; and (b) the fundamentals and the issues at stake.

If there is consensus at the community level of belief and on the fundamentals, and especially on the rules or principles, or both, for resolving conflicts, then it is much easier to manage conflicts.

While consensus may be close to unanimity, it does not consist of any one mind postulated by the monochromatic vision of the world but evokes the endless process of adjusting the many dissenting minds, as well as interests, into changing coalitions of reciprocal persuasion. This is to say that while "dissensus is the entropic state of social nature, consensus is not found but must be produced."[10]

In other words, the production of consensus in a crisis situation, characterised by irreconcilable positions or claims, is a creative art. And only those who are adept in the psychological understanding of human nature; those who can appreciate the complexities of rural life, its uniqueness and nuances; those who have the ability to identify a middle ground and build a consensus around it; and the ability to maintain this middle ground and gradually draw disputants towards it, can successfully mediate a crisis and produce consensus.

---

[9] This can be challenged by those who believe that legal knowledge can only be specialised knowledge – judicial officers know best. To this there are two possible answers: (a) that rural knowledge and legal knowledge need not necessarily be opposed, and (b) that legal problems of any sort are socially constructed.

[10] Amitai Etzioni, *The Active Society*, New York: Free Press, 1968, p. 470.

Analysis

In settling these disputes, some of the general principles earlier enumerated were applied where appropriate. In case number one, it was known that Okolie did not breach the contract between him and Maidor. Mr. Okolie was therefore not guilty of any offence. It was only accidental that the payment he made to Maidor's wife was not given to Mr. Maidor as obviously intended. The decision was based on the principle that guilt, and not accident, is what makes people liable. It was also clear that since there was a wrong, there must be a remedy. That remedy was found in a middle of the road decision which was consensually arrived at.

In the third case involving Chief Osu and Mr. Oseji, the decision was based on the principle that anger is not guilt; that both men were angry at each other's behaviour did not firmly establish guilt on either side.

In all ten disputes, the exclusion of the parties from the process of decision-making was to ensure that no person should be a judge in his or her cause. The use of jurors was intended to enhance objectivity, impartiality and truth. To ensure fairness, all parties were assembled together and at the same time. No party was heard in the absence of the other party. Each party gave evidence in the full view of the public and in the presence of the other party.

Witnesses also gave evidence in the presence of the parties to the dispute. These measures were intended to ensure fair hearing or due process. Finally, oath-taking by all the parties and their witnesses was also intended to ensure that truth prevailed.

Socially injurious alternative decisions were decidedly excluded in the process of decision-making. For example, in the dispute involving the sale of cassava plot, it would be socially injurious to allow the revocation of the sale when the instalments agreed upon were duly paid. Besides, the purchaser committed no offence in relation to the sale and the agreed mode of payment.

In the pregnancy dispute, it would be socially injurious to hold that Okoh's family did not have responsibility for the behaviour of their son, just as it would be socially injurious to hold that Mr. Dike ceases to have responsibility towards his daughter because of her behaviour.

In the blacksmith's dispute, it would be socially injurious not to recognise the status of a chief in public, just as it is socially injurious for a chief not to be humble enough to respect persons who are elders but not chiefs. The exclusion of these extremes that are socially injurious and implausible to the Igbo, enhances the mediation process.

In case number eight, it would be socially injurious not to punish Dilim severely as the council decided. It is not in the public interest not to make an example with Dilim's behaviour, and the council did just that. In case number ten, council simply re-emphasised the principle that the public interest is preferable to private ones. It would be socially injurious to decide otherwise.

Dispute settlement in Igbo is, therefore, not solely intended to enforce pre-existing rights, obligations, and duties but is strikingly conciliatory, informal, and non-adversary. Parties to a dispute are supposed to go away after judgement, not as mortal enemies, but as friends, neighbours and comrades once again. This feature of dispute settlement in Igbo appears missing in the modern Nigerian legal system. It even appears opposed to it because no conscious and determined effort is made by Nigerian courts to bring about reconciliation between parties to a dispute. Courts in Nigeria simply, strictly and mechanically, limit themselves to the enforcement of rights, duties, and obligations. They merely impose decisions on parties to a dispute. Reconciliation may be latent, but never focal.

There appears to be a distinction between civil and criminal offences. The former is in violation of private rights in connection with personal status, property and contract. To remedy the wrong that has been done reparation, restitution or compensation is instituted and compelled.

Criminal offenders (treason, theft, incest, witchcraft, sorcery) are fined (goats, cows, tubers of yam) but in the case of murder, the offender may be ordered to pay compensation to the victim's family. This may be in the form of the murderer using his son or daughter (depending on the sex of the victim) for such compensation; that is, the son or daughter of the murderer is given to the family of the victim as a kind of replacement.

Imprisonment was unknown but banishment was reserved and used for offences considered to be inimical to the public interest. Torture was relatively uncommon except in cases of witchcraft where it was employed as a means of making the suspect to confess.

The evidence most favoured in reaching a verdict is usually that of eyewitnesses. Circumstantial evidence and evidence based on hearsay are admissible, though they have little credence. They carry less weight in reaching a verdict one way or the other.

The knowledge of a person's character and pedigree is helpful in terms of determining the value to be placed upon the testimony given.

If a person's statement is doubted, the person is questioned extensively and this suffices to show whether that person is telling the truth. Those who bear false testimony and in the process mislead the council, are severely rebuked and punished.

Factors as provocation, negligence, or accident, the calibre of the individuals involved in a dispute, their relationship to one another, are important in terms of determining what reparation to award or the punishment to impose.

Whichever is the case, there is a concerted effort by everyone, particularly the council, to effect a reconciliation, the restoration of harmony being deemed more appropriate than the rigid adherence to the spirit and letter of the law. Council usually takes refuge in the popular proverb which instructs thus: let the lion eat, but at least leave the bones; that simply means we should not be too hard on people, on anyone.

The "reasonable man"

In case number ten, the use of the notion of the reasonable man was most clearly demonstrated. The unreasonableness of Nwaka's behaviour was magnified by rhetorically expanding the object of the dispute. In addition, palace officials talked of the duties and perceptions of a reasonable citizen:

a) a reasonable citizen will not violate communal interest;
b) a reasonable citizen will co-operate to restore communal interest when they have been violated.

In the others, the use of the notion of the reasonable man was not as clearly evident. Yet, it is implied in (a) the use of a jury to source decisions, (b) the open debate which takes place prior to the selection of the members of the jury.

Against this background, it would have been unreasonable to revoke the sale of the cassava plot because the buyer did not breach the contractual agreement pertaining to the sale. It would also have been unreasonable to hold that the owner of the cassava plot should not receive the full payment for his cassava *(case number one)*.

It would have been unreasonable to suggest that Dike had no more responsibility towards his daughter simply on the grounds that the daughter was impregnated by her boyfriend *(case number two)*. And it was reasonable to hold that Mrs. Okolo had far much greater responsibility to her sister and the children than any one else *(case number four)*.

These and the others are conceptual as well as material instances of what terms or conditions reasonable and informed men would agree to. They are the instances of the kind of statements and decisions reasonable and informed men would make.

It follows that something should be foreseen if a reasonable man would foresee it; an action is negligent if a reasonable man would refrain from it; bad if a reasonable man would not do it; an action is right because it is simply what a reasonable man already does. Sometimes, council refers, not to what a reasonable man would agree to, but to either how he would understand some idiom, phrase, proverb, question, or how he would regard the logic of some argument, or how he would react to a completely novel idea or situation.

It is clear, then, that the use of the notion of the reasonable man is a way of ensuring that contracts, statements, claims, and decisions are not stridently opposed to public morality, good conscience, and community wisdom. It is to ensure that decisions are not counter to an Igbo community's sense of impartiality, objectivity, truth, and justice. It allows standards of care to be adjusted to an Igbo locality.

The reasonable man notion is, thus, a rule that, because of its derivation from Igbo brotherly and fraternal notions of neighbours, of men and women of good conscience, justifies quite literally any decision arrived at while at the same time constraining the council.

The reasonable man is also a logical defence based on nothing but, at best, the council's perception of ordinary women and men. It is the viewpoint of the men and women in the street or those of right-minded men and women. It serves to justify decisions by presenting such decisions in terms of popular will or in terms of community wisdom.

The jury

In Aniocha Igbo, jury means *ume*. Trial by jury is concomitant with Igbo customary judicial ideology. It is an important ingredient in the arduous process of decision making, particularly decisions of a judicial nature. Trial by jury is the privilege and right of every Igbo adult; its healthy working only requires recognition by the common folk.

The Igbo jury system is not derived from any system, whether English or otherwise. It is not part of the received law which forms a significant part of the Nigerian legal system. It is not what it is because some law giver, indigene or foreign, decreed it. It is what it is because it is the way it has grown within the Igbo customary judicial system.

Indeed, its invention by a lawgiver is inconceivable. The Igbo are used to it and they know that it works because it embodies ideas that are neither ridiculous nor impracticable. Rather, it arises from the need for a wrongdoer to be judged by the community or neighbourhood. It is a way of making an individual accountable to the community for his or her misdemeanour. And for the Igbo, an individual must be willing to be judged by the community of which he or she is an integral part.

Most of the people selected for jury service are not educated in the western European sense of education. But they are not illiterates in terms of the knowledge of the custom and way of life of the community where they live. Because they possess this knowledge, they are the sole judge of fact as well as law.

Members are drawn from the community and are usually taken to have knowledge of: (a) community norms, values and ethos; (b) knowledge of all the relevant facts concerning a particular case; (c) men who are prudent, that is, those who are capable of deliberating and can calculate well with a view to some good end or ends.

Among the Igbo, there is no separation between judge and jury, because there is no rigid separation between fact and law or between morality and law. There is no difference in origin, between questions of fact and questions of law. The other reason is that power is diffused rather than separated.

Judges and jury are not conceived of as separate institutions, never any decision by any one or by the assembly of all adult male citizens that questions of law must be decided by "lawyers and judges", and those of fact by jurors who are ordinary lay men and women.

There were no lawyers and judges in the modern sense of these words in Igbo rural life. There are still none of these sorts of professionals engaged in conflict resolution in traditional Igbo setting. All that is required of a jury man is practical wisdom in the Aristotelian sense, that is, a reasoned and true state of capacity to act with regard to human good, and the ability to see what is good for themselves and for other human beings, in general.

Members of the jury derive their powers from the community and from the knowledge that the community will accept their suggested verdict if they have done a good job. The jury is thus a socio-legal and cultural instrument used by the community to enable it arrive at just, reasonable and right decisions.

The jury is representative of the community as a whole with one outstanding characteristic: the desire to see that justice is done, that justice is done *coram populo*. It is the micro community in relation to the communal need for justice in the peaceful resolution of conflicts. As a safeguard for the individual Igbo (guilty or innocent), the council ensures that those appointed or selected as jurors are unbiased, unprejudiced and independent.

The jury men, as the eyes and ears of the Igbo community, are the epitome of the reasonable man or woman, the ordinary man or woman in the village square, in the farm, in the market, street or at home. There is no special qualification other than that no one would be allowed to sit in judgement in a matter in which he/she has an interest.

As the eyes and ears of the community, they listen to the claims and counter-claims, the evidence adduced, the witnesses and the effect of the cross examination, and other members of the public (audience) who may have some contribution to make. Members are not engaged in any kind of professional ritual but help to give the ordinary Igbo man the sort of justice he can understand because it makes sense to him. It ensures that trial and punishment conform to the ordinary Igbo man's idea of what is fair, right and just.

The functions of judge and jury are fused rather than separated. Only the *obi* or *diokpa* is exempted from jury service because he is the Chairman of the council. Rather than being an instrument in the hands of a court, and perhaps kept at a subordinate position as in the English legal system, the jury in Igbo legal system occupies a pivotal position in conflict resolution, legal and non legal.

Jury verdict has legal as well as moral effect once judgement is entered upon it by the council. The jury's function has always been to answer the question: where does guilt lie? Or, who is the offending party? Judgement depends on its answer to these questions but not before compromise, in terms of give and take, on the part of all those engaged in dispute.

The jury's place in a trial has always been held in high esteem because of three reasons. First, wrongdoers should not be unpunished. Second, the voice of men is the voice of the gods and the ancestors: *onu mmadu bu onu chiukwu*. Thus, when the jury says that someone is guilty (for example) they mirror the position of the gods. The penalties demanded, the apologies, etc., are only minimal in comparison to the uncompromising demands of the gods and ancestors. Third, the task of fact-finding and webbing them together in order to establish guilt or innocence, cannot be done by the whole community. As a body of persons, they have to determine facts upon the evidence placed before them, suggest applicable law and sanctions for the guilty. In so doing, they are careful not to deviate from Igbo standards of objectivity, morality, law and justice.

At the end of proceedings in a particular case, the jury does not simply say yes or no as an answer to a question from any one. Instead, it suggests a line of reasoning which leads to judgment, and strenuously provides justification. It assiduously details its findings of fact and law. Upon its reasoning, the prestige and resilience of Igbo law, morality and justice, in great measure, depends.

The jury operates in the open. Members are not individually or collectively held incommunicado or sequestrated. They are members of the public who happen to be in the palace at that particular point in time. Members are thus never informed in advance. It is an abomination for some one to be informed formally or informally, of his selection for jury service in a matter he knows nothing about.

Part of the requirement for jury service is that those selected must be those who were in the palace when parties to a dispute presented their sides of an event, called their witnesses, and cross examined the witnesses of the other party, all these in an open court. Members must be, *ab initio,* part of all these in order to qualify for jury service.

Members, in order to examine the evidence before them, are allowed to retire into an inner chamber in the palace to brainstorm. Even in this, they are absolutely at liberty to communicate with any one, including litigants, in the presence of all. There is thus no formal obligation to secrecy in terms of what happened in the inner chamber or in the open court.

The decision of a jury is final only when given the stamp of authority by the council. While a jury is expected to produce a unanimous decision often based on the sense of the meeting, that decision is final only when it is adopted by the council. On occasions, where a jury is split, a new jury is immediately put together. Though rare, it does happen.

Under grave situations or conditions, the council can convert itself into a jury of the whole house. Under the circumstances, parties to a dispute are asked to momentarily take their leave, to enable council fruitfully deliberate and arrive at a decision.

The jury men are the purveyors of the kind of justice and order that the Igbo want to have and do cherish, not the sort experts think is good for them. Jury trial is a protection against tyranny, especially the tyranny of court officials and of some influential members of an Igbo community. In this vein, every jury is analogous to the assembly of adult male citizens, hence its sense and verdict is often seen as the people's sense and verdict.

Therefore, the jury in Igbo is far more than an instrument of a community in its attempt to see that justice is done. The jury is the lamp of liberty and freedom of every Igbo adult. Fundamentally, it is the lamp of the Igbo republican sentiment and has helped secure to every Igbo adult that trial by his neighbour which in the ultimate is the grand bulwark of liberty, freedom, truth, peace and justice.

An overview

What I have outlined so far from the foregoing is an analysis of the generic components of Igbo judicial process and the several domains that must be brought together before it can be said that justice has been done to an individual or the community.

The techniques which were used were often applied directly to cases or indirectly to one or more of the components of a decision. They can be briefly summarized as follows:

1. analogical extensions of judgements to relatively similar cases;
2. consistent application of espoused rules and principles enshrined in *omenani;*
3. imaginative and sympathetic consideration of alternative morally relevant outlooks in order to accommodate those which they have no good reasons for dismissing;
4. reflective equilibrium considerations to justify newly generated or modified principles and rule, if any;
5. seeking common ground for a shared social morality which is mutually revivified and reinforced;
6. negotiating compromises on outstanding differences to the extent that this is (a) possible and (b) morally admissible and acceptable;
7. building consensus on differences identified and agreed upon as basis for settlement;
8. dealing with residual non-negotiable differences by some other morally agreeable strategies;
9. attempting, as far as humanly possible, to find and establish the best alternatives in the relevant domain of settlement; and, finally,
10. reckoning with the fact that to know the good is not to do the good (Socrates), but rather to have a potential motive, however weak, in that direction. Such a motive, coupled with an understanding of

other facets of human nature, may lead to alliances with other motivational forces such as guilty feelings, social rewards, punishments, the tugs of conscience, and other means of making it more self-fulfilling to be good.

These are the rational resources, which are available for use in the settlement of different claims arising from the conflict of interests. These conflicting interests are not only normal but are necessary and sufficient grounds for our being in the world with others.

Chapter 7

Socio-cultural associations and the administration of justice

Introduction

These associations, often referred to as peer groups, are part of life in an Igbo community. An Igbo community is not complete without the existence of motley of these groups and subgroups. These groups serve a plurality of ends: economic, social, religious, cultural and judicial. Many of these ends converge to work out solidarity. Some may diverge.

Whether converging or conflicting with each other, none can be divergent from community interests in law, order, peace and justice, and survive for long.

A community needs the existence of these groups because membership in them fosters and encourages individualism, communalism, inter-dependence, cooperation, tolerance, and mutuality. In a culture that points to a vision of the world, based in essence, on the belief that likeness, not difference, consensus not dissent, make for good life, these groups play significant roles. They support communal life, render obedience to laws, and minimize the animosities among people who claim to share the same destiny.

These multiple associations, voluntary and non-voluntary testify to the developed state of interaction in an Igbo community.

The groups ensure the presence of crosscutting cleavages. When cleavages are crosscutting, they neutralize rather than reinforce each other because individuals have cohesion. The groups are mutually sustaining and reciprocally reinforcing agencies.

Apart from the specific purpose or purposes which the groups are meant for, they serve much more profound ends. They help to administer law and justice in the community. They assist in the management of conflict through the settlement of disputes between their members.

One striking characteristic of these groups is their specialized membership and function. While membership is open to all members of the community, training, specialization and competence in an aspect of community life are reckoned with in terms of a decision concerning membership. In principle, the Obi is the chairman of these groups because the Obi "owns" the land. In practice, each group has its own officials. Problems beyond their scope, administrative, cultural, religious, judicial, are referred to the Obi-in-Council.

Only fools are excluded from participation in the affairs of an Igbo community but women are not. Fools are excluded from membership of these groups and the political community because an Igbo proverb says that: if you tell a proverb to a fool, he will ask you its meaning.

Few women and more men have access to political participation and to the membership of these groups. For both sexes, public status is a matter of personal achievement. It is not by ascription. A woman's status is determined, not merely by that of her husband, but by her own achievements too.

Kinds

The groups are many. The following are only representative samples of them.

Izu uzu

This is an association of blacksmiths. It is exclusive to males. They discipline their members when need be.

Izu dibia

This is an association of medicine men, diviners, soothsayers, sorcerers, psychiatrists and orthopaedic surgeons. It is exclusive to males. They have the responsibility of ensuring the mental, spiritual, and physical health of members of the community. They deal with all kinds of sicknesses and diseases, of the mind or the body, or both. They have exclusive jurisdiction over issues concerning witches and witchcraft. Besides, they also engage in the resolution of disputes between their members.

Izu omu

This is the association of women charged with the overall welfare and discipline of women in the community. While some men are members, the women outnumber them. Some of the members, especially women, are traditional medicine practitioners, skilled in mid-wifery - ante and post-natal care - and other aspects of female disease management, care and cure.

Their leader, called *omu,* occupies a powerful political, religious, social, cultural and judicial political position in the community. The judicial powers exercised in her court (collectively) are important and fairly enormous.

Most female offences and offenders are first dealt with, directly, in her court. Those who are dissatisfied in her court, take their cases to the council.

Its activities help to further womanly character and virtue. For example, a woman who consents to sexual intercourse in the afternoon and in the bush, or in forbidden places like sacred grooves, shrines, etc., is subject to disciplinary measures, after due process. So is a woman proven to have engaged in gossip, or to have secretly watched her husband making love to her mate (husband's second or third wife), or who has used language unbecoming of a woman. Upon conviction on any of these offences or similar ones, the penalty for a married woman is heavier and much more severe. The jurisdiction of this group covers the activities and life styles of all women, members and non-members.

The association's functions may be divided into two related parts: (a) self-rule among women; and (b) articulation of women's interests as opposed to those of men. It provides women with a forum in which to develop their political talents, and a means of protecting their interests as traders, farmers, wives, mothers and widows through collective action against individual women or men, and men as a group.

It makes rules about markets and enforces them. It exerts pressure to maintain moral norms among women and men too. It listens to complaints from wives about mistreatment by their husbands. The converse also applies. It makes decisions about rituals concerning the women aspect of the community's guardian deity. Particularly, it makes decisions about rituals required to protect and enhance the fertility of the womb and of the soil.

While the *omu* association served the function of articulating and protecting women's interests, it is more than a pressure group. It shared in the diffused political authority characteristic of Igbo communities. It also shared in the diffused legal authority as well. There is thus a case for what Okonjo called the bisexuality of Igbo political and legal systems.[1] This means that there is a dual system of male and female political, legal and even religious institutions, each with its own autonomous sphere of authority and influence.

Speaking generally of women, Forde and Jones observed that

> "women's associations express their disapproval and secure their demands by collective public demonstrations, including ridicule, satirical singing and dancing, and group strikes.[2]

The *omu* association occupies a unique position in the community. It is at the apex of women groups and associations. It has the responsibility of organizing women in order to achieve goals considered important and desirable by the womenfolk.

By virtue of her position, the *omu* is a member of some other important associations in the community, for example, the council, *izu dibia, izu inwene.* Besides, these associations also engage in dispute resolution between members and between them and non-members.

Izu okpala

This is the association of all titled men, especially those who have performed the *okpala* chieftaincy title. All of them are members of the

---

[1] Kamene Okonjo, "Political Systems with Bisexual Functional Roles – The Case of Women's Participation in Politics in Nigeria," paper presented at American Political Science Association Annual Conference, Chicago, 1974, p.25.

[2] Daryll Forde and G.I. Jones, *The Ibo and Ibibio Speaking Peoples of South Eastern Nigeria,* London: International African Institute, 1950, p. 21.

council in the *obi*'s palace. From among their members, the *obi* forms his inner (kitchen) cabinet. Prominent among them are those who hold special chieftaincy titles like: *odogwu, iyase, isama, oza,* etc. This association is exclusive to the male members of the community.

Izu inwene

This is the association of all women who have performed the *inwene* chieftaincy title. It is exclusive to women. It is the female equivalent of the *okpala* title for men. It is charged with the discipline of its members and women in general.

Izu onotu

Odogwu, the war commander of the community, is their leader. The *odogwu* is equivalent of a modern day chief of army staff, because the *obi* is the commander-in-chief. Membership is drawn from other associations, for example, *Izu dibia* and *Izu Uzu.* This group is charged with the responsibility of taking care of the farm land (fertility ceremonies), murders (victims and murderers), suicide (successful and unsuccessful), sacred grooves, the forest in general, and the defence of the community in the event of war. Women are excluded from membership of the group.

For example, those who successfully commit suicide are buried by members of this group after the rituals intended to cleanse the land have been done. Suicide, it is held, pollutes the land and this affects the fertility of the land. Those who are unsuccessful are punished by the group after the necessary rituals. Besides, they also discipline their own members when the need arises.

Otu ogbo

These are the age-grade associations. Apart from their social responsibilities, they also discipline their members and help to implant the virtues of cooperation and loyalty. They foster the communal spirit when they engage themselves in community related public works, like cleaning the village square, weeding the footpaths leading to the village stream or communal farm land. Because membership is open to all adult citizens, all youths, male or female, age-grade associations help to promote friendship, cooperation and mutual dependence between the sexes. Membership of these associations cuts across lineage and socio-economic standing in the community. Membership is not hereditary, though some families have, over a long period of time, acquired the reputation of being known to be competent in blacksmithing, traditional mid-wife doctors, rain doctors, sorcerers, and orthopaedic surgeons.

Some of the special titles like *odogwu, iyase, isama,* may belong to a lineage. But this does not mean that such a title would then be the exclusive property of a family in that lineage. The title remains non-hereditary while the lineage from time to time decides who among them is best qualified to hold the title.

The objectives of these associations described above are practical as well as ideal. In the case of disputes between members which defy amicable settlement within a particular association, the final court of appeal is the council. Occasionally, though not always, such an appeal may be heard first, in the assembly of the leaders of all the peer groups before finally reaching the council. In very delicate situations (delicate as defined by the council but not hinged on the self interest of any body), the council may subtly engineer its intervention in order to prevent disorder and chaos. In all conflict situations, the usual methods of and mechanisms for dispute settlement are put in place.

Specialization

These socio-cultural associations are made up of individuals who, by their training and other special circumstances or qualifications, are best suited for the tasks necessitated by their membership. Most of the members are experts in matters relating to their area of specialization.

Besides the specific expertise in each association, they ensure that members live up to their oaths of office. Discipline is strictly maintained within each association and infractions are punished.

In this connection, it is clear that these associations work essentially in the interests of the community. The ends they seek and other activities undertaken under their aegis have social approval whether or not the activities are intended to serve some communal purposes or for the benefit of individual members of the public. They function to propagate values that are socially relevant to the issues concerning law, order, justice and peace in the community.

Overview

What these considerations imply is that the role of these associations is, to a large extent, similar to that of a national institution performing various kinds of public functions.

Their relevance lies in the fact that they normally have codes of conduct for members. They lay down rules of conduct and prescribe certain forms of behaviour for members. New or prospective members are screened and those known to have skeletons in their cupboards are rejected.

The rules laid down usually take the form of prohibitions, and infractions are believed to affect some kinds of actions and social relationships.

Some of these prohibitions have the effect of a moral code whose infractions are supposed to produce psychological and physical consequences, not only for members but also for the members of their families, and the community itself.

The primary functions of these associations can be summarized as follows:

a) to maintain law and order;
b) to administer justice;
c) to organise defence against external enemies;
d) to protect the community from its internal enemies;
e) to conserve unappropriated natural resources;
f) to manage public utilities, for example, roads and markets and
g) to provide other services like recreation and relief for the poor
   members of the community.

In conclusion, the Aniocha Igbo community owes much to the variety and the partial autonomy of these socio-cultural organizations, each of which makes its own distinctive contribution to the administration of justice in the community. If there is a fundamental pattern of contribution, it is presented in a varied surface and perhaps richer in terms of each organization's uniqueness.

The contributions are at two related levels: (a) their insistence on obedience to and compliance with their own rules and regulations; and, (b) their insistence on obedience to and compliance with community rules and regulations, in general.

These socio-cultural organizations, thus, help to strengthen the ties that hold the community together by ensuring that their members are law abiding, and are not deprived of much to which they are accustomed. They ensure that the machinery for enforcing laws and regulations within them and in the community itself are not undermined by reckless and unscrupulous members within their fold.

Even though civil discord is concomitant with community life and is perhaps an irremediable disease of life in general, the organizations help to maintain a balance between the need for public order and the demands of the individual to do as he/she pleases.

Chapter 8

Legal pluralism

Complementary community systems

The Igbo belong to two distinct but complementary community systems: the micro one which is theirs and thus, natural to them, and the macro one which is the Nigerian system "artificially" created as a result of a political act – the amalgamation of the Northern and Southern Protectorates of Nigeria in 1914.

This means that they are subject to the laws of Nigerian society as well as the *iwu obodo* as enshrined in their *Omenani*. It means they have to wilfully and consciously serve two masters simultaneously: double compliance with the dictates and requirements of *Omenani* and the demands of citizenship as enshrined in the Nigerian constitution which is the supreme, basic law of the land.

This double compliance raises the issue of legal pluralism. This pluralism is not to be regarded as something unique and novel *per se,* because other forms of pluralism are part and parcel of Igbo life viz: religious, political, philosophical, linguistic, etc.

Igbo law *(iwu obodo),* is an example of an informal and unofficial legal system developed by the people for many centuries. It seeks to establish social stability and community survival. It is informal because there are no recording officials, no elaborate ceremonies as in a modern state. It is official and formalised in terms of the demands, requirements, and imperatives of *Omenani.*

Igbo law does not claim to regulate social life outside Igbo areas, nor does it question the criteria of legality prevailing in the larger Nigerian society. Both legal systems are based on respect for the dignity of human persons, good behaviour and the substantive principles of private property.

The informality and flexibility in Igbo judicial system is achieved through the subtle use of the principles, discussed in chapter five, in its entire system, though some of these principles are not very different from those in the Nigerian legal system. Thus, although both occupy different positions along a continuum of formalism, they share the same legal ideology. These principles outlined in chapter five are of considerable relevance in both legal systems in terms of their use in conflict resolution.

Legal reasoning in both systems is dominated by rhetorical elements directed towards different goals. The rhetoric in Aniocha Igbo is directed towards restructuring broken relations and how to mend them while the Nigerian system concerns itself with who is legally right or wrong, and the award of punishment. In both systems, there is some degree of uncertainty and probability which cannot be removed by any deductive or apodictic reasoning. One of the ways of dealing with this problem is to take refuge in an invective art. That is, to find points of view or to rely on principles which, being widely current, acceptable, and reasonable, help to fill the gaps.

This has one advantage which is most profound: it renders the reasoning convincing and the conclusion acceptable. The degree of acceptability differs because in the Igbo system, decisions or conclusions are consensually arrived at, while in the larger Nigeria system, decisions or conclusions are impositions of standards based on a written formula. The conclusions in the Igbo system are also an embodiment of standards and values which are not consciously and wilfully imposed, *(see Diagram 4 at p.177)*.

The decisions in the Igbo system are the product of consensus and mediation. While the impositions are not statutorily supported and binding, public opinion, some times, helps to enforce compliance on the part of individuals.

Diagram 4 explains the relationship between the two systems: Igbo and Nigeria. The Igbo system is spacious because it is a subtle combination of mediation, adjudication, the imposition of decisions, and the invocation of Nigerian standards and values when morally and legally convenient. Cases 7, 8 and 10 in Chapter Six lucidly exemplify this trend.

The Igbo system is unofficial because it is not authorized or confirmed or formally approved by the relevant organs of a modern state. Unlike the Nigerian state system, its legality is not a matter of legislative Acts.

The Nigerian state system, as per *diagram 4* is an adjudicatory and adversary system. It is official because it is properly authorized. It is invested with the aura of officialdom, is documented and validated by reference to legislative Acts.

Legal pluralism

The unquestionable assumption is that the Nigeria legal system, at least, represents in substantial form, the interests of its citizens. However, there is a situation of legal pluralism which is structured by an unequal relationship in which Igbo legal system is the subordinated part thereof.

Igbo legal system may be regarded as an exemplification of the communalist spirit in a Nigerian capitalist socio-economic framework as reflected in its laws. It is an example of a communalist system (forcefully) integrated into a capitalist world, though the degree and success of the integration effort is debatable. The Igbo system is still very much alive though attenuated by decades of colonial and post colonial problems of the Nigerian state.

Although the Igbo system is not markedly exemplified by the influence of antagonist's social classes, their existence is undeniable. The social stratification is not as antagonistic as in the overall Nigeria state system because of the underlying ideology of communalism. Viewed loosely, the Igbo system is social democracy at the primordial level and thus untainted by class struggle.

The Nigeria state has tolerated the Igbo system, as it is at present, because it is functional to its interest as a polity. By disposing of secondary conflicts among the Igbo, its system, not only relieves the official Nigerian courts, but also reinforces the socialization of the Igbo. By providing the people with peaceful means of dispute settlement, Igbo system neutralizes potential violence, enhances the possibility of orderly life and thus instils a respect for law and order that carry over when the people interact with the larger Nigerian society.

These are achieved at no financial burden to either side of a dispute, unlike the high litigation costs borne by litigants in official courts in Nigeria. The political authorities in both systems do find that the preservation of law, order, justice, and peace promotes the good life of the citizenry.

There is an element of adaptation in the Nigerian legal system which is absent in the Igbo system. To a large extent, some aspects of the Nigerian system are part of the received (imposed?) law from England. The principles analysed in chapter five are, however, not part of it. These principles, from an Igbo point of view, have been adapted and integrated into the official Nigerian system with a capitalist bent. This situation of legal pluralism is a reflection of past subordination, and a structure of colonial domination.

That the Nigerian state has tolerated the Igbo system this far is no guarantee against future intervention and the threat of that intervention remains, if and only if, Igbo system does not run counter to the demands of law, order, justice, and peace in the Nigerian system. The threat remains to the extent that Igbo system can be declared repugnant by the Nigerian official court system.

Unofficial legality

In a traditional situation, unofficial legality is one of the instruments which is used by the local people to organise community life and enhance the socio-economic well being of their community.

The political evaluation of unofficial legality, thus, depends upon the community in whose name it operates and the goals at which it is directed. What appears, therefore, on the surface, to be ideological conformism is not more than a realistic evaluation of the constellation of forces and the concrete needs of Igbo community.

Where this unofficial legality deviates from the Nigerian system, it can be considered as a strategy for community survival. Thus, while the two systems share the same legal ideology, they put it to very different uses because the goals are different.

The inversion of the basic norm of property, for example, is not a deviation from the Nigerian system. But the selective use of legal formalism through which a folk system of formalism has evolved, is discernible. Informalism, in general, is a function of the absence of professionalism in the modern sense, low level of differentiation and stratification, and little or no specialization.

The specific operation of informal rules, the ways in which they are created, affirmed, refused, changed, adulterated, neglected or forgotten, is a function of social objectives, general cultural postulates, ideas of legality and justice.

Among the Igbo, the main function of formalism is to guarantee the security of property and persons, the certainty of moral, social, and economic relations without violating the overriding interest of a system of justice that is accessible, quick, intelligible, and reasonable to the people.

Legal skills

Legal skills in Igbo are widely distributed. Thus, many Igbo people perform what can be regarded as law jobs in a non-professional manner. Professionalism in law and in social reality, and of knowledge, in general, has been closely associated with the development of modern societies.

In traditional Igbo society, there are professionals in medicine, politics, literature, poetry, etc. There are no professional lawyers and judges in the modern sense of these terms. All that is required is knowledge, native intelligence, and practical judgement, especially knowledge of the nuances of Igbo culture and tradition.

In Igbo community, as in any other traditional system, the relation between power and knowledge is very obvious. The dialectic of power and knowledge is concretised through anecdotes. But because professionalism in the legal domain is not institutionalised, legal skills are readily available because they are widely distributed.

Without professionalism there is no monopoly of legal knowledge or of the legal system as in the Nigerian state. With the monopoly of legal knowledge and system; parties in dispute, unlike what obtains in the Igbo system, are first alienated and second, denied their legal and judicial needs.

In both systems neither party has full, complete, and absolute control of the legal process. However, parties in Igbo system have considerable leeway to speak for themselves, interact directly with the other person or persons, and the witnesses. This represents a clear-cut contrast with the Nigerian legal system where lawyers who (claim to) know best speak and act for and on behalf of the parties in dispute. The parties are, thus, onlookers in a drama in which they were, *ab initio*, the *dramatis personae*. Legality in the Nigerian state means the construction of alienation, the transformation of the familiar into the unfamiliar, the gift into the burden, the innocent into the guilty, and the just into the unjust through the application of and reliance on the technical knowledge of law and the legal process.

This technical knowledge and process is absent in the Igbo system and even when it is present, it nowhere approaches the extremes which characterise the official legal system of modern Nigerian state.

Powerlessness of individuals

The problems which people encounter daily are not understood in legal terms and so, taken away from them as in the Nigerian system. People can solve these problems directly because their fears, worries, desires and interests are not translated into legal terms and concepts. Neither are these fears, worries, desires, etc., treated as legal terms and concepts. Because these problems are faced directly by those who encounter them, Igbo legal system responds to the legal needs of individuals rather than the converse where the autonomy of individuals is subsumed under the autonomy of the system.

Community wisdom and knowledge are not sacrificed on the altar of technical knowledge, which ultimately renders persons powerless. The powerlessness of the ordinary person can be indicated in two ways. First, through the claim that the world is constituted in a particular way and that nothing can really be done to change it even when change is obviously desirable. Second, through the insistence that what change can come about must come through a certain class of people in society: the experts and their surrogates.

In law, this is transformed into the doctrine that lawyers, judges and other judicial officers know best. Law, then, regulates the kind of changes that are possible and denies power to the ordinary person by claiming that it and the experts who service it, know best.

These are manipulative structures within which there is a quiet flight from the truth, but it is the truth that legal systems ought to seek in all matters and manners of dispute. Truth is life: *Ezi okwu bu ndu,* is perhaps foreign to the official Nigerian legal system, just as the system is foreign to the people.

Although we are accustomed, in common language, to speak of the pursuit of truth in a manner which suggests that the aim of all rational investigation is the truth, a little reflection will show that this is a case where common speech is apt to be philosophically misleading, especially in the official Nigerian justice system, a system that nourishes the divorce between truth and justice because of its reliance on technicalities.

The Igbo system achieves the subtle conflation of truth and justice because for them, there cannot be one without the other. Truth is something that exists rather than something that can be created and recreated in the process of resolving a dispute. For them, there is no unbridgeable chasm between truth and justice, whereas in the Nigerian official system this chasm exists, and is created and recreated in the courtroom drama in which only experts are allowed to speak, argue, and cross-examine litigants and witnesses.

The court, thus, forces people to accept its own definition of reality. This takes place within the context of a judicial epistemology that divorces the human from the world. It claims that the legal world is a world of immutable, ahistorical, atemporal facts distinct from human activities.

The legal system in Aniocha north local government area, Delta State

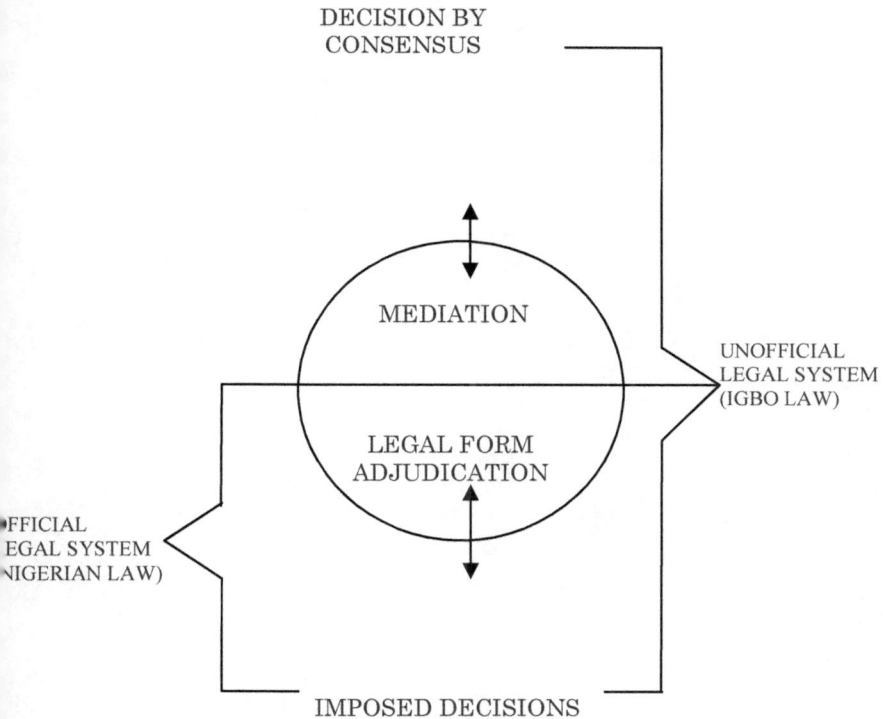

DECISION BY
CONSENSUS

MEDIATION

LEGAL FORM
ADJUDICATION

UNOFFICIAL
LEGAL SYSTEM
(IGBO LAW)

OFFICIAL
LEGAL SYSTEM
(NIGERIAN LAW)

IMPOSED DECISIONS

Diagram 4

Chapter 9

The end of justice in Igbo community

Introduction

Nature has a purpose, so has society and its institutions. Life has a purpose or end, so is death. Polygamy serves a purpose, so is the rule of exogamy and the extended family system.

In the same vein, a rule, principle, norm or convention is made or invented to serve a purpose or a plurality of purposes. An idea has an end which it is intended to serve. It has an aim, intention or purpose. In general, human acts are purposively oriented.

Justice, as an idea, a principle or norm, must have an aim, an end, intention or purpose. What then is the end or purpose of justice in an Igbo community?

As Okafor suggests "the Igbo seek and cherish justice in all spheres of activities."[1] The Igbo cherish justice, not only for its own end, but also for the ends which it serves.

These ends may be briefly summarised as follows:

i) to restore social equilibrium or balance disrupted by bad conduct of any kind;
ii) to repair and readjust a relationship which has been fractured by such bad conduct, between two or more persons, and between individuals and the community;
iii) to reconcile and reunite parties to a dispute;
iv) to restore relationships and in the process re-emphasise the communal bond;
v) To reintegrate the offender into the mainstream of social life and existence;

---

[1] F. U. Okafor, *The Igbo Philosophy of Law, op. cit.,* p. 40.

vi) To emphasise the spirit of co-operation, dependence, mutuality and reciprocity, thus making it clear to everyone that human life is not it without the others who are in the same boat of life with us;

vii) To apportion desert and punish offenders. Punishment is neither for the fun of it nor ostensibly to alienate. Instead, it is to drive home a salient point, that is, that there is reward for work done or not done, either here or hereafter or both;

viii) To ensure as well as promote the good and well-being of persons and the community;

ix) To promote order, peace, justice, good and effective management of community affairs; and

x) To safeguard and guarantee the security of persons and property. Property and contract are not safeguarded and guaranteed at the expense of persons, yet attempts are made to safeguard and guarantee all through a balancing act that may not always be satisfactory.

Interdependence

The Igbo concept of a person has been minimally affected by the twin effects of Christianity and western European education. So is Igbo community ethos and life style. The emphasis is still largely on corporate and communal life, on patrilineal descent and the definition of a person's status, role, political, legal, moral rights, and obligations through membership of the community. According to D. Forde:

> "In a material culture in which the technological development does not allow for specialization, one has to rely on many people."[2]

Forde's position raises the problem of interdependence, which means that people are not regarded as independent and equal. Instead, relationships are interpreted to imply the elements of dependence and the inequality implicit in it.

Dominating the relations between individuals is the whole pattern and scheme of mutuality, co-operation, and the long run reciprocities in the social structure.

---

[2] D. Forde, ed, *African Worlds,* Oxford: University Press, 1954, p. 188.

One tree cannot make a forest; therefore co-operation is required for the tasks and problems of life. The security of life and property is bound up with the mutuality of kin, cognatic, agnatic, and affinal.

Wealth is not despised if it is the result of hard work but it is not focal in a relationship. Life is valued more than wealth: *ndukakwu.* Life itself is regarded as a special form of wealth: *ndubuakwu.* It is the concern for the other which is manifested in caring, sharing, co-operation, and helpfulness, not the display of wealth that is focal.

The emphasis on sharing, on give and take, and on dependence is motivated by unavoidable necessity of promoting, sustaining and maintaining the good life for every member of the community. The cultivation of life, which is based on give and take, on live and let live, the absence of professionalism in the legal domain, the lack of an overpowering coercive power in the socio-political structure, conjunctively make consensus, moderation, compromise, and mediation the keynote of Igbo life.

Divergent interests

Naturally, there are conflicts arising out of the pursuit of divergent interests, the imperfections and limitations in the trado-social institutions or in their inadequacy in satisfying all the needs of members.

In the resolution of conflicts, arbitration and compromise are pre-eminent in terms of their subtle employment, morally and judicially. The genius of a legal system, even in its most informal and unprofessional aspects, is the ingenious use of the restitutive sanction. In the main, the fundamental purpose is the re-establishment of relations that have been fractured and strained. This objective is achieved, not by the vindication of extant rules, but by vigorous attempts directed towards reconciling the parties. There is the assumption that social equilibrium will be continually maintained to the extent that relations between persons are adjusted and readjusted in the most suitable manner.

The primary problem, as usually perceived by the *Obi*-in-council, is the necessity of smoothening the edges of a fractured relationship and in the process, smoothen out personal difficulties. The task before them is not to settle legal issues or to restore pre-existent legal rights and privileges. This may come about during the process of mediation. It may come about as the unintended consequence of the mediation process.

According to the Igbo in Aniocha, law and rules are not more important that the personal relations which the rules are supposed to order. Edward Levi has shown that in law "the dominant element is the resolution of a problem, not the system."[3] Levi may have had the American legal system at the back of his mind, but his thesis applies, with equal force, to all kinds of legal systems that are engaged in the resolution of problems.

Individual choice

The mediative, compromising, and conciliatory tone of conflict resolution does not foreclose individual choice. In the process of conflict resolution, parties have considerable leeway to disagree with the final outcome. As a consequence, full latitude is allowed them to expostulate. If the council of elders thinks that a genuine grievance exists, the issue is revisited in order to make for an amicable settlement which is the end of justice.

The overriding idea is that since *Omenani* exists for the good of human beings, it is not an end in itself. Since it is only a means to an end, duties, rights, and obligations between individuals and groups are predicated on their formal agreement.

If there is no agreement between individuals, there can be no relationship; a relationship easily becomes a makeshift. If coercion is the rule rather than the exception, there can be no genuine, fruitful agreement. This explains why the implementation of a decision is often left to the parties in dispute. The entire socio-political structure relies on the maintenance of good relationship that is achieved without compulsion. The extended family system, membership of age-grade groups, and membership of other sub-groups, ties individuals together into an intricate network of relationships. These help to foster the ideals of common fate, common destiny, and corporateness. These in turn lubricate the wheels of good relations between members of a community.

Great importance is attached to the dignity of the individual and high value is placed on human life. Hence, if a party to a dispute

---

[3] Edward Levi, *An Introduction to Legal Reasoning*, Chicago: University Press, 1949, p. 45.

expresses dissatisfaction with the outcome, the right to complain is exercised to the fullest.

There is an obligation to complain because as an Igbo proverb puts it, 'the air (fart) that is still locked in a stomach cannot foul the environment: *awulu dina afo odi esi isi.* The right and obligation to complain and seek redress is not a one sided affair. The community is obligated to listen because *ani nwe obi, obi nwe ani:* the *obi* is the people just as the people are the obi. One without the other is meaningless.

Good conduct is relative to the human condition and morality is oriented, not from absolute standards, but from the point of view of the community good in each concrete situation. Conduct that promotes, enhances and sustains relationship and thus upholds the community structure, is good; while conduct that is opposed to these aims is bad.

To say that conduct is oriented, not from absolute moral standards, is not an endorsement of moral relativism. It is only to take account of the place of historical and cultural diversities in the moral domain. Igbo communities subscribe to the universality of some moral norms – like the prohibitions against incest, murder, theft, etc., without which a community cannot function, and without which the ideals of a community may not be realized. The sanctions for bad conduct are, first and foremost, the pressure of public opinion and of reciprocal arrangements of the political and social structure. An individual thus conforms to *Omenani* because of self esteem and the premium placed on reputation for fairness, truth, objectivity, moderation, and the ability to get along with others, not only among the kith and kin, but also in the wider circle of friends and neighbours.

Reconciliation and the possibility of restitutive sanction are part of the great forces at play. The imperatives for social life of co-operation, everyone's dependence upon day-to-day mutualities, immensely exert an irresistible pressure on parties to the dispute to carry out compromises reached in a settlement. Without compromise justice is, perhaps, unattainable.

Igbo communities are distinguished because of their republican form of life. This was a feature that was not understood early by the British colonial administration.[4] The exercise of power has never been

---

[4] A.E. Afigbo, *An Outline of Igbo History*, Owerri: Rada Publishing Co., 1986, p. 16. Afigbo examined the problems closely associated with the lack of understanding of Igbo political system, specifically the Igbo, east of the River Niger. Interestingly, his findings and conclusions are germane to the issues raised in this chapter, as well as the Igbo in Aniocha north local government area of Delta State.

the result of transformation of unconditional right into a permanent object of struggle among competing groups in which the quest for identity, the quest for a politically stable understanding and organization could be separated from the experience of communal living.

This republicanism entails openness, which is a necessary condition for the kind of inclusive, cosmopolitan nature of Igbo communities. A significant part of what it takes to keep this democratic arena open is willingness to respond to the claims of others who are not immediately recognized as one of their own kind. The distinctive character of this republican community lies in the opening of a public space in which the community may come to speak, not with any particular voice, but with a heterogeneous multiplicity of voices. No one is ever forced into silence.

This multiplicity of voices prevents any singular, dictatorial or absolute justification of the republican adventure in terms of a transcendental ground to which all could appeal. Though any Igbo community may claim the heritage of republicanism for itself, offering a justification in terms of the authority of its interpretation of its value and significance, none may ever, in the ultimate, appropriate it. The republican fate of all such attempts is to remain contested, up for question in the public space they claim to determine, but which must finally escape all such determination.

Power lies essentially in the assembly of all citizens and it is in the large concourse of Igbo adults that policy decisions are taken, decisions about the welfare of the citizens and the security of the community. The decisions of the assembly are executed by the *Obi*–in–council.

Behind these social and political structures is the ancestor gods and *Ani* (the earth goddess). There is a close relationship between the ancestors, morality and justice. The ancestors are the guardians of morality, law and justice. It is they who visit on their descendents punishment for some act or omission. In the case of the community, it is *Ani* that visits punishment on particular individuals or on an entire community for some act (*Nso ani,* that is, abomination, offences against the land) or omission.

Conclusion

There was never an attempt to unearth the unfamiliar or the unknown in this research work. Of course, one would have been happier if this had happened. If anything, the findings are not pedestrian. The findings restated, perhaps in a new form, and in a much more vigorous manner, the thesis that whenever human beings congregate there must be law and order. Wherever human beings are found there must be law and order. Infractions are punished in accordance with the tradition of the human group in question. These appear to be one of the irreducible minimum requirements for the survival and flourishing of the human species.

It is ideological to posit or argue that there can be a human group that has no system of reward, no sense of justice and its cognates, and no sense of revulsion against wrongdoing or injustice of a sort. It is ideological to acknowledge the existence of the system of law and government but down-grade the same on the grounds of an assertion of difference and cultural superiority.

If anything, there are no two social systems or cultural systems that are commensurable. On epistemic and other grounds, cultural systems are incommensurable. So are standards of measurement. There is no Archimedean point with which to make any evaluative comparisons between varying cultural practices.

As I concentrated my research on the dispute settlement mechanisms associated with the Igbo, I came to conceive of these mechanisms and their institutional setting as forming an unofficial legal system which I called Igbo law. I then analysed this law in its dialectical relations with the Nigerian official system as an instance of legal pluralism.

This perspective saved me from the temptation to study Igbo as an isolated community, a serious short-coming of most legal studies of this kind. Furthermore, I employed a class analysis, examining legal pluralism as the relation between a dominant legal system (the official Nigerian legal system) and a dominated system (the Igbo legal system).

The unofficial, dominated system has been presented, not as a forum to which a litigant may appeal from an adverse decision under Igbo law, but as a threat aimed at reinforcing the decision of the council under that law. Thus, the threat is not overtly aimed at alienation but it is a subtle manoeuvre towards compliance, conciliation and reintegration.

Traditionally, Igbo justice system has been hinged from time immemorial on humanness. Reconciliation, reintegration and social harmony achieved through mediation are the goal of its legal institutions rather than punitive measures and imposed decisions. To achieve reconciliation, council's job is not limited to guiding the disputants to reach a compromise solution of their differences. Rather than play a passive role, council plays an activist role in seeing that this reconciliation is genuinely achieved.

Drawing from the ideas and concepts enshrined in *Omenani,* the Igbo grundnorm, I identified some basic principles of Igbo law. I also identified some basic structures of reasoning and argumentation, and correlated them with other features of the socio-cultural life.

It is a socio-cultural life in which it is an accepted fact that the community has powers that are irreducible *vis-a-vis* those of individual members. But this is not an insurance against deviance in one form or the other, since at any given time one or more individuals may express less than absolute conformity to the rules of proper conduct.

This concern with the community, that it is supreme, is not merely intended to smoothen Igbo society's way of life and pattern of existence or to ensure the consistency of these traditional patterns. It is intended to continually revivify belief in Igbo collective destiny – a destiny that has no meaning outside the idea of acting and working together for a common purpose. Above all, it is intended as a way of maximizing human welfare.

This is the prevalent, extant socio-cultural milieu in which conflicts not only occurred, but must necessarily occur, a milieu in which disagreements must necessarily take place. It is a milieu that has no shortage of legal skills in an uninstitutionalised legal framework. This apparent lack of institutional arrangement was what (a) shocked the colonial administration, (b) misled its officials into the false assumption that the Igbo have no kings: *Igbo enwene eze*.[1] In the Aniocha area, there are kings in every community.

From this assumption, the conclusion that the Igbo have no legal system was drawn. The argument is flawed on one serious note. Lack of an institutionalised political and legal framework did not result from lack of a centralised kingship system. The lack of both never meant the absence of law and order.

To fill the wrongfully perceived gap the British colonial administration in a proclamation order of 1900 created native courts. These courts were empowered by law to adjudicate on customary matters. In 1956, a reform bill replaced the native courts with customary courts.

In establishing these courts in Aniocha area, the colonial government, through the District Officer (D.O.), was careful to locate them within the three clans of the area: Ezechima, Odiani and Idumuje. The customary court for Ezechima was initially located at Onitsha-Olona but later relocated to Issele-Ukwu. That for Odiani was located at Ukwu-Nzu, while the one for Idumuje clan was located at Idumuje-Unor.

Initially, these courts were presided over by the District Officer who was resident at Ogwashi-Ukwu, the then headquarters of the district of Aniocha as a whole, that is, the present Aniocha north and south. As time went on, the District Officer was replaced by the indigenes of the area where a court is located.

In implementing this reform, other problems were created. The earliest indigenes to acquire western European form of education were the slaves, servants and the never-do-wells in the localities. These groups of people were also the early converts to the Christian faith. For most Igbo aristocrats and "freeborn", only these groups of Igbo people were good enough to have any contact with the white man. It was from this group that the early catechists, teachers and interpreters were employed. This was understandable, because these were the only people who understood the white man. They spoke the white man's language.

It is interesting to note that withdrawal from, or perhaps, momentary total rejection of the "other" – *wa*, who is not like us – *anyi*, is not strictly European in origin, though with them, this gradually became racist. It appears to be perfectly human and thus, natural.

However, when the colonial government decided to employ members of this group as presidents and members of customary courts,

---

[1] For an interesting discussion on this enigmatic claim, see Prof. M.A. Onwuejeogwu, *Igbo Nwere Eze*, (Igbo have kings), Benin City: Mindex Press, 2002, pp. 1-64.

the indigenes protested, and did so vehemently. It was inconceivable that members of this group should: (a) preside over the Igbo aristocrats and the "freeborn" in the community; (b) as members of the customary court they took decisions concerning them; and (c) they took precedence over them in public because of their new positions.

It was a violation of Igbo norm to have one man, who was not appointed by them in an assembly, to represent them in any capacity. It was worse if such a person should give orders to everyone else. It was worst in a situation where such a person or persons had to adjudicate rather than mediate in conflicts between brethren.

The officials of the native courts were obeyed when they had to, since the power of the colonial government was behind them. People avoided using the native courts when they could do so. Cases could be forced into the courts and fines imposed for infractions of rules.

By having the ear of the colonial administration, the officials of the native courts could violate local customs and traditions and get away with it since their version of events and of reality would be believed eventually.[2]

Add to these abuses was the overbearing power of the court clerks. Though employed as servants of the court and the people, they gradually became the masters. They re-defined court protocols, and dominated court proceedings because of their monopoly of one important resource and expertise: literacy.

The direct consequence of the reform was that the customary court system suffered a credibility problem right from its inception. For, apart from the criminal offences that were taken away from the palace of the *Obis*, it was business as usual. The councils in the palaces functioned as if nothing has happened. Indeed, it did not matter to the indigenes that there was a new court system. Even in criminal matters, parties to a dispute, in most cases, settled at home without the knowledge of the customary court or the colonial administration.

The introduction of income tax was resented. It came with its own problems, one of which was that enumeration for census was mistakenly linked to a head count of those eligible to pay tax.

Worse still, tax defaulters were forcibly arrested, taken away, and arraigned before customary courts for trial and conviction. To apprehend the defaulters, there were tax raids in villages which were

[2] J.C. Anene, *Southern Nigeria in Transition, 1885–1906*, New York: Cambridge University Press, 1967, p. 259.

organised by the officials of the native authority. The elderly and the able bodied men were forced to unceremoniously relocate to farm huts in order to escape arrest. The raids were resented because they dislocated family and communal life.

The trials neither met nor approximated Igbo standards of impartiality, objectivity, truth, fairness, and justice. The indigenes felt scandalised, insulted and psychologically assaulted on the grounds that they were compelled to listen to and obey people who, in the Igbo traditional scheme of things, have not washed the hands with which they ate food with the vultures, that is, those who are really nothing. And such people were not likely to be able to wash those hands. Furthermore, the trials lacked the human touch which characterised the Igbo justice system.

The introduction of the native police force and court messengers to help in the administration of law and order did not help matters. Again, the calibre of people employed to do the job, the method they used in doing their job, the way and manner they carried on and presented themselves did not encourage the indigenes to give the new justice system that came with customary courts any chance to succeed.

These factors made the customary court unpopular, and patronised only when they were forced to. Lack of patronage from those the court was designed to serve immobilised it. The high handedness of its officials was equally matched by the resentment of the indigenes. The social status of its officials meant that neither the court nor its decisions earned the respect of the indigenes.

This was the setting when independence was proclaimed in 1960, an event which brought its own innovations and problems.

Since independence the Igbo traditional justice system has been further formalised with the establishment of customary courts and the customary court of Appeal of a State.[3] Section 282(1) of the 1999 Constitution states that the Appeal Court shall exercise appellate and supervisory jurisdiction in civil proceedings involving questions of customary law. The supervisory function presupposes the existence of lower courts, i.e., customary courts.

The unused and untested 1989 Constitution was peculiar in one significant aspect. The Fourth Schedule, Part I, Section 8, created traditional councils and enumerated their functions. It specifically took

---

[3] (a)Chapter VIII, part II, C, of the 1979 Constitution of Nigeria.
   b) Chapter VII, part II, C, of the 1989 Constitution of Nigeria.
   c) Chapter VII, part II, C, of the 1999 Constitution of Nigeria.

away executive, legislative and judicial powers from the *Obi*-in-Councils.

It was not exactly clear whether the traditional council and the *Obi*-in-council are intended to be functionally equivalent. They are not. Perhaps, it was meant to be the equivalent of the council of chiefs at the state level.

The customary courts in the pre-independence period were manned by the indigenes of the area who have knowledge of their own culture and tradition. These officials were unprofessional lawyers and judges. Since independence, the key officials of these courts are professionally trained lawyers and judges.

While the "modern" customary courts are staffed with professionally trained officials, there is still a preponderance of unprofessional legal staff who function in some of the courts.

Whereas the *Obi*-in-council, in conjunction with adult members of the community, listen to litigants and thereafter arrive at consensually equitable decisions, the modern customary courts are replications and imitations of the official Nigerian court system where the determination of justice depends on the wisdom of one, two or three persons.

There are four features that characterise the modern Nigerian court system. It does not share these features with the Igbo traditional justice system. The features are:

a) adjudication rather than mediation;
b) imposition of decisions;
c) all-or-nothing decisions; and
d) winner takes all decisions.

These features are absent from the Igbo justice system. They are even opposed to Igbo system which is itself characterised by consensual decisions arrived at through the mechanism of mediation. The fundamental difference is, indeed, not the problem for Igbo justice system today.

There is a gradual and systematic erosion and diminution of the effectiveness of Igbo justice system today. While several factors can be held to account, the most important ones are, without much controversy, western European education and Christianity.

The democratization of access to education has had liberalising and liberating effects. Ignorance about nature and ourselves is gradually disappearing. The walls of prejudice and bias concerning the way things are, are gradually breaking down. Many Igbo minds are consequently being liberalised and liberated from fear, ignorance, prejudice, etc. The old order is changing, even if, reluctantly and slowly.

Today, if one is not willing to go to the *Obi*'s palace to defend or institute a suit, nothing is probably going to happen. Nothing perhaps will happen. For one thing, such suits are certainly civil ones. They cannot be criminal. Persuasion is the only method for winning people over. Persuasion backed with ostracism was fearsome. The effects were no more dreaded.

Ostracism is now weakened in the Igbo system because the worldview of the average Igbo has undergone some radical transformation through the influence of formal education.

Christianity, for all its colonial and neo-colonial trappings, has meant that many Igbo Christians would rather die than swear to something or anything they regard as a fetish object like *ofo*. For those Christians with a liberal disposition, swearing to the Bible in order to proclaim their innocence rather than *ofo,* is acceptable.

The combination of formal education and Christianity has, to a considerable extent, devalued Igbo traditional justice system. While the effects of the devaluation are obvious, it is certainly not the case that the Igbo system is about to disintegrate.

This conscious devaluation of the Igbo justice system represents a micro dimension in the entire process. The truth is that the Igbo culture and tradition in its wholeness is being devalued, weakened and destroyed. Igbo morality and traditional beliefs are being grossly undermined. Defiance against the principles and laws of the Igbo as enshrined in *Omenani* has been overtly encouraged, particularly by the teachings and dogma of Christianity.

According to Chiegwe,

> "the cumulative effect of modernization, urbanization, formal education and Christianity on the local people has been insidious. Faith in the traditional beliefs and morality has been undermined, minds have been unsettled or poisoned against their indigenous culture, and defiance has been encouraged, and refusal to invoke a deity to arbitrate in a dispute has been encouraged."[4]

---

[4] Onwuka Chiegwe, "Disturb the Dead and Pay the Price: The Reverse Side of the Modernization Coin," *Africa,* Vol. LVII, No. 4, Dec. 2002, pp. 505 and 510.

It is obvious that Igbo justice system is under attack. While it is yet to collapse, disintegrate and disappear, it is clear that its life span wholly depends on the Igbo themselves in terms of their attitude to their cultural heritage, and their response to contemporary changes in Nigerian society.

Bibliography

Works cited

Igbo studies

Afigbo, A. E., *An Outline of Igbo History,* Owerri: Rada Publishing Co., 1986.
Davids, P. K., *The Text Book of Igbo Proverbs,* Onitsha: University Publishing Co., 1980.
Edeh, E.M.P., *Towards Igbo Metaphysics,* Chicago: Loyala University Press, 1985.
Ifemesia, C., *Traditional Human Living Among the Igbo: An Historical Perspective,* Enugu: Fourth Dimension, 1980.
Njaka, E.N., *Igbo Political Culture,* Evanston: North Western University Press, 1974.
Nwala, T.U., *Igbo Philosophy,* Lagos: Lantern Books, 1985.
Okafor, F.U., *Igbo Philosophy of Law,* Enugu: Fourth Dimension, 1992.
Williamson, K., *Igbo–English Dictionary,* Benin City Ethiope Publishing, 1972.

African studies

Dike, K.O., *Trade and Politics in the Niger Delta 1830–1885,* Oxford: Clarendon, 1956.
Forde, D. ed., *African Worlds,* Oxford: University Press, 1954.
Mbiti, J.S., *African Religions and Philosophy,* London: Heinemann, 1982.
Nwanunobi, C.O., *African Social Institutions,* Nsukka: University Press, 1992.
Obiechina, E., *Culture, Tradition and Society in the West African Novel,*

Cambridge: University Press, 1971.

Parrinder, E.G., *African Traditional Religion*, London: S.P.C.K., 1962.

Schapera, I., *Government and Politics in Tribal Societies*, New York: Schochen, 1967.

Anthropology

Mair, L., *An Introduction to Social Anthropology*, Oxford: Clarendon, 1975.

Marett, R.R., *Anthropology*, London: 1912.

Radcliff-Brown, A.R., *Structure and Function in Primitive Society*, London: Kegan Paul, 1976.

Law and justice

Bohannan, P., *Justice and Judgement Among the Tiv*, London: Oxford University Press, 1957.

Fellers, L., *Law without Precedent: Legal Ideas in the Action in the Court of Colonial Basoga*, Chicago: University Press, 1969.

Gluckman, M., *The Judicial Process Among the Barotse in Northern Rhodesia*, Manchester: University Press, 1955.

Kantorowicz, H., *The Definition of Law*, Cambridge: University Press, 1958.

Levi, E., *An Introduction to Legal Reasoning*, Chicago: University Press, 1949.

Pound, Roscoe, *Social Control Through Law*, New Haven: Yale University Press, 1942.

Other works

Baker, E., *Principles of Social and Political Theory*, Oxford: University Press, 1967.

Etzioni, A., *The Active Society*, New York: Free Press, 1968.

Paton, H.J., *The Good Will*, London: Allen and Unwin, 1927.

Perelman, C., *The New Rhetoric: A Treatise On Argumentation*, Notre Dame: University Press: 1965.

Articles

Abel, R.L., "A Comparative Theory of Dispute Institutions in Society," *Law and Society*. Vol. 8, 1973.

Agu v. Ikewibe, (1991) 3 NWLR.

Elombi, G., "Customary Arbitration: A Ghanaian Trend Reversed in Nigeria,"

African Journal of International And Comparative Law, Vol.5, No.4, 1993.

Gulliver, P., "Introduction to Case Studies of Law in Non-Western Societies," Laura Nader, Ed., *Law in Culture and Society,* Chicago: Aldine, 1969.

Onwuejeogwu, M.A., "An African Indigenous Ideology: Communal Individualism," Inaugural Lecture Delivered December 15, 1986, University of Benin, Benin City.

Otakpor, N., "The World is a Market Place," *Journal of Value Inquiry,* Vol. 30, No. 4, 1996.

_____ "A Sense of Justice", *Readings in Social and Political Philosophy,* Vol. 2, F.A. Adeigbe, ed., Ibadan: Claverianum Press, 1994.

_____ "Social Theories and Communal Ideology", *Dialogue and Humanism,* Vol. 1, No. 1, 1994.

Recasens-Siches, L., "The Logic of the Reasonable as Differentiated from the Logic of the Rational," R.A. Newman, ed., *Essays in Jurisprudence in Honour of Roscoe Pound,* Indianapolis: Bobbs-Merrill, 1962.

Pound, R., "Making Law and Finding Law," *Ohio Law Reporter,* Vol. 13, 1915.

Index

www.ingramcontent.com/pod-product-compliance
Lightning Source LLC
Chambersburg PA
CBHW021100210326
41598CB00016B/1274